POLITP9-CKO-581

Politics by Other Means

POLITICS BY OTHER MEANS

The Declining Importance
of Elections in America

BENJAMIN GINSBERG
MARTIN SHEFTER

Basic Books, Inc., Publishers

NEW YORK

Library of Congress Cataloging-in-Publication Data

Ginsberg, Benjamin.
  Politics by other means: the declining importance of elections in
America / Benjamin Ginsberg, Martin Shefter.
      p. cm.
  Includes bibliographical references.
  ISBN 0–465–01973–0
  1. Political participation—United States.   2.   Political parties—
United States.   3.   Elections—United States.   4.   Governmental
investigations—United States.   5.   Mass media—Political aspects—
United States.   6.   United States—Politics and government—1977–
I.   Shefter, Martin, 1943–   .   II.   Title.
JK1764.G56   1990
322′.042′0973–dc20   89–43090
                                                                              CIP

Copyright © 1990 by Basic Books
Printed in the United States of America
Designed by C. Linda Dingler
90 91 92 93 RRD 10 9 8 7 6 5 4 3 2 1

For our families

Contents

Preface

STRUGGLES OVER POLITICAL ETHICS dominated the first year of the Bush presidency. Democrats blocked the confirmation of John Tower as secretary of defense by accusing him of excessive drinking, sexual misconduct, and conflicts of interest. Shortly thereafter, allegations of financial impropriety pressed by Republicans against House Speaker Jim Wright and Democratic Whip Tony Coelho compelled both to resign from Congress. Congressional Democrats then brought charges of financial irregularity against House Republican Whip Newt Gingrich, prompting an Ethics Committee investigation of his personal finances and political fund-raising activities. Subsequently, congressional Republicans clamored for the resignation of influential Democratic Representative Barney Frank, who acknowledged involvement with a male prostitute.

These conflicts had a major impact upon the conduct of American government. To avoid a repetition of the Tower affair, the White House began to subject potential appointees to such exhaustive background checks that hundreds of high-level positions in the executive branch remained unfilled during much of the administration's first year. At the same time, Congress's preoccupation with the ethics of its leaders brought the legislative process to a virtual standstill.

George Bush won an overwhelming victory in the 1988 presidential election, but his ability to function as chief executive was impaired because he could not expeditiously fill important policy-making positions in his administration. Similarly, the Democrats won 60 percent of the seats in the House of Representatives in the 1988 congressional elections, but their ability to control the legislative agenda was seriously damaged by the Wright affair and subsequent controversies over congressional ethics. In both instances, forces defeated in the electoral arena deprived the winners of many of the fruits of victory.

The Tower, Wright, Gingrich, and similar affairs illustrate an important new development in American politics. Observers generally regard elections as the decisive events in American politics and devote much attention to assessing their meaning and significance. However, American politics has recently undergone a fundamental transformation: Other forms of conflict have grown in importance relative to electoral competition. Rather than seeking to defeat their opponents chiefly by outmobilizing them in the electoral arena, contending forces are increasingly relying on such institutional weapons of political struggle as legislative investigations, media revelations, and judicial proceedings to weaken their political rivals and gain power for themselves.

Many seemingly disparate political events of the past decade illustrate this transformation. The persistence of enormous budget and trade deficits, the continual allegations of misconduct lodged against high government officials, and pitched battles between the president and Congress over Supreme Court and executive appointments are all expressions of the diminished role that elections play in American politics. In conjunction with declining electoral competition and voter participation, these developments signal the emergence of a "postelectoral" political order in the United States. *Politics by Other Means* analyzes the origins and character of this new political order.

In writing this book, we received useful comments and suggestions from a number of colleagues to whom we would like to express our thanks. David Vogel took time out from his own work to read and criticize a draft of the entire manuscript. Preliminary versions of portions of our analysis were presented at meetings of the American Political Science Association and at a conference at the Institute for Governmental Studies, University of California/Davis, and were published as the following: "A Critical Realignment? The New Politics, the Reconstituted Right, and the Election of 1984," in *The Elections of 1984,* ed. Michael Nelson (Washington, D.C.: CQ Press, 1985); "Institutionalizing the Reagan Regime," in *Do Elections Matter?* ed. Benjamin Ginsberg and Alan Stone (Armonk, N.Y.: M.E. Sharpe, Inc., 1986); and "The Presidency and the Organization of Interests," in *The Presidency and the Political System,* 2nd ed., ed. Michael Nelson (Washington, D.C.: CQ Press, 1987).

We are especially grateful for the comments we received on these preliminary papers from Larry Berman, Walter Dean Burnham, Bruce Cumings, Alan Ehrenhalt, John Ferejohn, Thomas Ferguson, Peter Gourevitch, J. David Greenstone, Gary Jacobson, Stephen Krasner, Michael Nelson, Kevin Phillips, Frances Fox Piven, Nelson Polsby,

Austin Ranney, Michael Paul Rogin, Theda Skocpol, and Stephen Skowronek. Our colleagues at Cornell—Glenn Altschuler, Michael Goldfield, Theodore J. Lowi, and Jeremy Rabkin—offered a good deal of worthwhile advice. Martin Kessler, president and publisher of Basic Books, gave us the benefit of his sound editorial judgment. Charles Cavaliere, our project editor at Basic Books, supervised the book's production with consummate skill. Our thanks also to Kym Fraser, who prepared the charts and figures, and to Marie Bruce, for cheerfully typing and retyping large portions of the manuscript.

This book is in every sense jointly authored. Every argument was discussed, written, and revised by the two of us. For their forbearance during our collaboration, we are indebted to our families—Sandy, Cindy, and Alex Ginsberg; Sudy and Elizabeth Shefter. We are indebted to them for much else besides.

Politics by Other Means

1

Electoral Decay and Institutional Conflict

FOR MUCH OF AMERICA'S HISTORY, elections have been central arenas of popular choice and political combat. In recent years, however, elections have become less decisive as mechanisms for resolving conflicts and constituting governments in the United States. As a result of party decline and deadlock in the electoral arena, political struggles have come more frequently to be waged elsewhere and crucial choices more often made outside the electoral realm. Rather than engage voters directly, contending political forces have come to rely upon such weapons of institutional combat as congressional investigations, media revelations, judicial proceedings, and alliances with foreign governments. In contemporary America, electoral success often fails to confer the capacity to govern; and political forces have been able to exercise considerable power even if they lose at the polls or, indeed, do not compete in the electoral arena. As the twentieth century draws to a close, America is entering what might be called a *postelectoral era.*

The use of institutional weapons of political combat is not without precedent in American history; but over the past two decades, the importance of these weapons has increased while the significance and decisiveness of elections has diminished. This development has profound consequences for the nation's domestic affairs and international economic and political standing. Because contemporary elections fail to establish conclusively who will—or will not—exercise power, conflict over this question continues to rage throughout the political system. This exacerbates the historic fragmentation of government in the United States, further weakening the American state and making it difficult to achieve collective national purposes. Contending political groups are increasingly able to seize portions of the state apparatus and pursue divergent and often contradictory goals even in the face of serious domestic problems and international challenges. In short, a good deal of the difficulty America has recently faced in maintaining its position in the world is attributable to its politics.

FROM ELECTORAL TO
INSTITUTIONAL COMBAT

Several trends in contemporary American political life bring into focus the declining significance of the electoral arena and the growing importance of other forms of political conflict. American elections in recent decades have been characterized by strikingly low levels of voter turnout and the disappearance of meaningful competition in an increasing number of races. As figure 1.1 indicates, turnout in national elections has declined by 25 percentage points over the past century. In the 1988 presidential election, barely 50 percent of the eligible electorate went to the

FIGURE 1.1
VOTER TURNOUT IN PRESIDENTIAL AND
CONGRESSIONAL ELECTIONS, 1892–1988

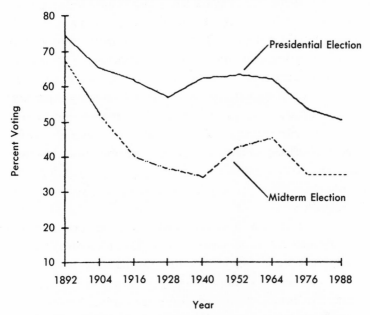

SOURCE: 1890 to 1958, Erik Austin and Jerome Clubb, *Political Facts of the United States Since 1789* (New York: Columbia University Press, 1986), 378–79; 1960 to 1988, *U.S. Statistical Abstract* (Washington, D.C.: U.S. Government Printing Office, 1989), 258.

polls; in the most recent midterm congressional election, the rate of participation was a mere 35 percent. In other Western democracies, turnout typically exceeds 80 percent.[1]

The extent to which genuine competition takes place in the electoral arena has also declined sharply in recent decades—especially in congressional races, which have come to be dominated by incumbents who are able to use

3

the resources of their office to overwhelm any opponents who might present themselves.[2] In 1986 and 1988, 98 percent of the incumbents who sought another term won reelection.[3] A majority of congressional races are now decided by more than a 20-point margin; frequently, incumbents face no electoral challenge whatsoever.[4] The absence of competition in congressional elections—which had once characterized only the South—is now becoming a national phenomenon (see figure 1.2). Incumbents also have a substantial (albeit less overwhelming) advantage in Senate races. Presidential contests are considerably more competitive than congressional elections. However, both the decisiveness and significance of presidential results has eroded in recent years.

As competition in the electoral arena has declined, the significance of other forms of political combat has increased. One indication of this displacement of conflict from the electoral arena is the growing political use of a powerful nonelectoral weapon—the criminal justice system. Between the early 1970s and the late 1980s, there has been more than a tenfold increase in the number of indictments brought by federal prosecutors against national, state, and local officials (see figure 1.3). Many of those indicted are lower-level civil servants, but large numbers have been prominent political figures—among them more than a dozen members of Congress, several federal judges, and numerous state and local officials. Many of these indictments have been initiated by Republican administrations, and their targets have been primarily Democrats. But a substantial number of high-ranking Republicans in the executive branch—including presidential aides Michael Deaver and Lyn Nofziger, and National Security official

FIGURE 1.2
THE ABSENCE OF COMPETITION
IN CONGRESSIONAL ELECTIONS

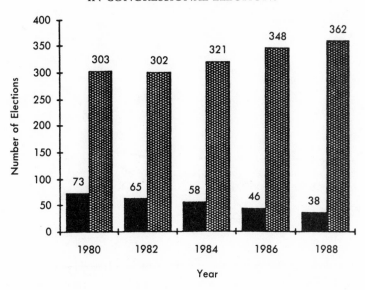

SOURCE: 1980, *Congressional Quarterly Weekly Report,* vol. 38, no. 45 (8 Nov. 1980): 3339–45; 1982, *Congressional Quarterly Weekly Report,* vol. 40, no. 45 (6 Nov. 1982): 2817–25; 1984 and 1986, *Statistical Abstract of the United States* (Washington, D.C.: U.S. Government Printing Office, 1988), 241; 1988, *Congressional Quarterly Weekly Report,* vol. 46, no. 46 (12 Nov. 1988): 3301–7.

Oliver North—have also been the targets of criminal prosecutions stemming from allegations or investigations initiated by Democrats. The data reported by figure 1.3 understate the extent to which public officials have been subjected to criminal proceedings in recent years, because they do not

FIGURE 1.3
FEDERAL INDICTMENTS AND CONVICTIONS
OF PUBLIC OFFICIALS, 1970–1986*

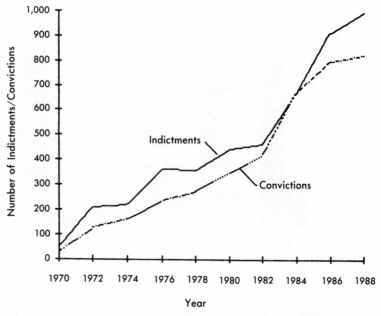

SOURCE: Annual reports of the U.S. Department of Justice, Public Integrity Section, 1971–1988.
*Reporting procedures were modified in 1983, so pre- and post-1983 data are not strictly comparable.

include those political figures (such as Ronald Reagan's attorney general Edwin Meese and Democratic House Speaker Jim Wright) who were targets of investigations that did not result in indictments.

There is no reason to believe that the level of political corruption in the United States has actually increased tenfold over the past decade and a half; but it could be argued that this sharp rise in the number of criminal indictments of government officials reflects a heightened level of public concern with governmental misconduct. However, both the issue of government ethics and the growing use of criminal sanctions against public officials have been closely linked to struggles for political power in the United States. In the aftermath of Watergate, institutions were established and processes created to investigate allegations of unethical conduct on the part of public figures. Increasingly, political forces have sought to make use of these mechanisms to discredit their opponents. When scores of investigators, accountants, and lawyers are deployed to scrutinize the conduct of a John Tower or Jim Wright, it is all but certain that something questionable will be found. The creation of these processes, more than changes in the public's moral standards, explains why public officials are increasingly being charged with ethical and criminal violations.

The number of major issues that are fought in the courts has also sharply increased in recent decades, further revealing the importance of nonelectoral conflict in America's current political system.[5] The federal judiciary has become the central institution for resolving struggles over such issues as race relations and abortion and has also come to play a more significant part in deciding questions of social welfare and economic policy.[6] The suits brought by civil rights, environmental, feminist, and other liberal groups seeking to advance their policy goals increased dramatically during the seventies and eighties—reflecting the willingness and ability of these groups to fight their battles in the judicial arena. For example, as figure 1.4 indicates, the number of civil rights cases brought in federal courts doubled during this period. After the emergence of a conservative majority on the Supreme Court in 1989, forces on the political right

FIGURE 1.4
CIVIL RIGHTS CASES BROUGHT IN FEDERAL COURTS

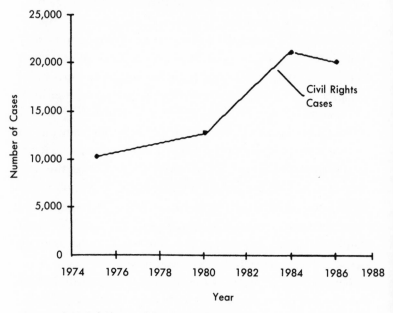

SOURCE: *Statistical Abstract of the United States* (Washington, D.C.: U.S. Government Printing Office, 1988, 1989), 172, 180.

formulated plans to use litigation to implement their own policy agenda.

Finally, the national security apparatus has been used as a political weapon in recent decades. One of the best-documented examples of this phenomenon is the substantial expansion that took place during the 1960s and early 1970s in the number of domestic counterintelligence operations directed against groups opposed to the policies of the executive branch. Such activities included wiretaps, surveillance, and efforts to disrupt the activities of these groups.[7] During the 1970s, congressional opposition brought a halt to this particular set of counterintelligence efforts; however, recent revelations have indicated that in the 1980s the FBI placed under surveillance groups opposing the Reagan administration's policies in Central America. The administration also came to rely upon the national security apparatus to circumvent and undercut congressional resistance to its policies.

PARTY DECLINE AND ELECTORAL DEADLOCK

Most analyses of American politics assume the primacy of elections. But elections are political institutions, and their significance cannot be taken for granted. The role played by elections has varied over time, and these shifts must be understood in the same terms as changes in the role and power of other institutions. Over the course of American history, political actors have undertaken to transfer decision making on a number of major issues from the electoral to other arenas, such as administrative agencies, the courts, and, in the Civil War, the battlefield. Indeed, forces defeated at the polls have not been averse to using other institutions they control to nullify electoral results. For example, during the late nineteenth and early twentieth centuries, middle- and upper-class "reformers" in American cities were at times able to use state legislative investigations, newspaper exposés, and judicial proceedings to drive from office the machine politicians whom they were unable to defeat through the ballot box.[8]

The declining significance of elections in contemporary America is a product of the electoral deadlock that has

9

developed in the United States over the past quarter century. The duration and scope of this deadlock are without precedent in American history. For eighteen of the twenty-two years between 1968 and 1990, neither the Republican nor the Democratic party was able simultaneously to control the presidency and both houses of Congress. Moreover, for twelve of the eighteen years that the Republicans controlled the White House during this period, the Democrats held majorities in both the House and the Senate.

This deadlock is linked to the decay of America's traditional partisan and electoral institutions. That decay began in the Progressive era, accelerated with the events surrounding the presidencies of Franklin D. Roosevelt and Lyndon Johnson, and has resulted in the virtual destruction of local party organizations and a sharp decline in voting turnout rates.[9] Of course, the Democratic and Republican parties still exist. But they have essentially become coalitions of public officials, office seekers, and political activists; they lack the direct organizational ties to rank-and-file voters that had formerly permitted parties to shape all aspects of politics and government in the United States.

The decay of party organization is a major theme in analyses of contemporary American politics.[10] Political scientists have attributed to it declines in voter turnout, increased electoral volatility, and a diminution in the accountability of public officials to voters. But in focusing on the effects of the decline of party *within* the electoral arena, analysts have paid insufficient heed to its implications for the relationship *between* elections and other political institutions.

Generally speaking, strong party organizations enhance the significance of elections, while declines in party strength reduce the importance of electoral processes. Inasmuch as their influence derives from the electoral arena, political parties are the institutions with the largest stake in upholding the principle that power should be allocated through elections. Thus, a diminution of party influence and an increase in the power of other political agencies is likely not only to reduce the relevance of elections for governmental programs and policies but also to allow electoral results themselves to be circumvented, resisted, or even reversed by forces that control powerful institutions outside the electoral realm.

In contemporary American politics, party decline has fostered a stalemate in the national electoral arena and encouraged contenders for power to look elsewhere for weapons to use against their political foes. This deadlock has stemmed from the differential impact of the decay of political parties, and the decline of electoral turnout that has resulted from it, on congressional and presidential elections. With party decline, personal organization and name recognition have become critical in low-visibility elections such as those for the House of Representatives. In a variety of ways, Democratic candidates have gained an advantage in these realms. Republicans have the advantage in high-visibility presidential contests, where issues and ideology are of prime importance. The decay of political parties has reduced voter turnout, especially among low- and moderate-income groups, resulting in a heavily middle-class electorate—44 percent of those voting in the 1988 presidential election had family incomes above $35,000 a year—increasingly concerned with its tax burden. GOP presidential candidates have been able to appeal more effectively than their Democratic opponents to this predominantly middle-class electorate.

In congressional elections, the first advantage that the

Democrats derive from party decline and low levels of turnout has to do with incumbency.[11] The growth of split-ticket voting that has accompanied party decline enables incumbents to build personal bases of support for themselves and to retain their seats even when the other party's presidential candidate sweeps their district. Moreover, the ability of incumbents to draw upon the resources of the federal government for electoral purposes is an especially important factor when only 35 percent of the eligible electorate votes. The overwhelming advantage House and, to a lesser extent, Senate incumbents have come to enjoy has contributed to the Democrats' ability to perpetuate the congressional majorities they first built during the 1930s and renewed in their 1964 and 1974 electoral landslides.

Because of the resignation, retirement, and death of incumbents, three to four dozen congressional seats become vacant in each election year. However, the Democrats maintain an advantage in races for open seats, winning roughly 60 percent of these contests in recent years. One reason Democrats have been able to do so well is that they have a stronger base in state and local government. This base gives the Democrats an advantage in the drawing of congressional district lines. It also provides them with a pool of experienced and visible elected officials available to compete for open House and Senate seats.

Another source of the Democrats' advantage in congressional elections is their ability to draw upon the support of thousands of individuals who are affiliated with local governments and nonprofit organizations and who are prepared to work for candidates committed to domestic programs and expenditures.[12] This support grows more valuable as party organizations and voting turnout decline.

In the presidential arena, by contrast, the decline of party organization and voter turnout has weakened the Democrats and strengthened the Republicans. Groups committed to higher levels of domestic spending and other liberal causes play a major role as campaign workers and contributors, caucus participants, and primary voters in the Democratic presidential nominating process. With the collapse of party organization, Democratic candidates for the White House have become heavily dependent upon these groups to conduct and finance their primary campaigns. The appeals that candidates must make to compete successfully for the party's presidential nomination, however, often undermine their chances in the general election by permitting the GOP to portray them as being too liberal.[13] Such portrayal can be extremely damaging in presidential general elections. Here ideology and national issues play a much larger role than in congressional contests, where voters are mainly concerned with protecting narrower interests.[14]

The issue of race confronts Democrats with a particularly acute version of this problem. Black voters overwhelmingly favor the Democrats, and that party's presidential candidates have become heavily dependent upon this support in general elections. In fact, the Democrats have received more than 20 percent of their votes from blacks in recent presidential contests. Though there is little danger that these voters will defect to the Republicans, the Democratic party's chances of victory in presidential races can be seriously impaired if blacks do not come to the polls in large numbers. To maintain high levels of black voter turnout, the Democrats must focus on such issues as civil rights and social programs. Unfortunately for the Democrats, these appeals have alienated large numbers of blue-collar white voters in the North and South who, since the 1960s, have become increasingly dissatisfied with the party's stands on racial questions.[15]

The Democrats' dilemma has been exacerbated by the growing political prominence of Jesse Jackson, who has energized and won the ardent support of millions of black Americans. Jackson's influence over the black electorate has enabled him to demand, as a condition for his urging blacks to vote, that the Democrats accord him a prominent role and focus on issues of concern to his constituency. To the extent that they meet these demands, the Democrats risk losing even more support among those whites who are wary of the party's stance on race. In 1984, the Democratic presidential nominee Walter Mondale was impaled on one horn of this dilemma when he aggressively courted black voters and lost substantial support among these whites.

In 1988, Michael Dukakis sought both to placate Jackson at the Democratic national convention and at the same time to avoid the appearance of having made substantial concessions to him. This effort was doomed to failure, and Dukakis found himself caught on both horns of the Democrats' racial dilemma. Many whites, believing that the Democrats had once again shown too much concern for blacks, supported the Republicans. Blacks, for their part, were convinced that Dukakis had not been sufficiently attentive either to Jackson or to their political interests more generally—convictions that Jackson did little to dispel. As a result, black voter turnout dropped from its 1984 level.[16] This combination of white defection and black nonparticipation was a central factor contributing to Dukakis's defeat in the 1988 presidential election.

The only way the Democrats can overcome their racial impasse is to develop issues and programs that attract voters across racial lines, most likely by devising programs that appeal to blacks and whites on the basis of common economic concerns. Such a strategy was employed by nineteenth-century European social democratic parties, which succeeded in uniting workers by imbuing them with a common class identification.

The ability of the Democrats to employ a social democratic strategy is limited, however, by the reality that low levels of voter mobilization leave America with an overwhelmingly middle-class electorate, which is unlikely to be sympathetic to such appeals. Proposals from Jesse Jackson and others that the Democratic party take steps to register and mobilize large numbers of new minority and low-income voters have met with a cool response from many established party leaders and public officials. They fear that a massive influx of new voters might further heighten the party's racial dilemma, drive middle-class voters into the Republican camp, and threaten the party's control of offices it currently holds. Without significant expansion of the electorate, however, efforts to win elections by uniting white and black voters are not likely to succeed.[17]

These factors help to explain why the Republicans prevailed in five of six presidential elections between 1968 and 1988, while the Democrats continued to dominate House elections and usually won control of the Senate during these same years. In effect, the decay of America's traditional electoral structures has permitted each of the major contenders for power to establish an institutional stronghold

15

from which it cannot easily be dislodged through electoral means.

INSTITUTIONAL COMBAT

Party decline and electoral stalemate have had critically important consequences for the locus of political combat in the United States. Of course, the Democrats and Republicans continue to contest elections. But rather than pin all its hopes on defeating its foes in the electoral arena, each party has begun to strengthen the institutions it commands and to use them to weaken its foe's governmental and political base.

President and Congress

The Republicans continue to enter candidates in most congressional races but have reacted to their inability to win control of Congress by seeking to enhance the powers of the White House relative to the legislative branch. Thus, President Nixon impounded billions of dollars appropriated by Congress and sought, through various reorganization schemes, to bring executive agencies under closer White House control while severing their ties to the House and Senate. Presidents Reagan and Bush tolerated budget deficits of unprecedented magnitude in part because these precluded new congressional spending; they also sought to increase presidential authority over executive agencies and diminish that of Congress by centralizing control over administrative rule making in the Office of Management and

Budget. In addition, Reagan undertook to circumvent the legislative restrictions on presidential conduct embodied in the War Powers Act.

The Democrats, for their part, compete vigorously in presidential elections but have responded to the Republican presidential advantage by seeking to strengthen the Congress while reducing the powers and prerogatives of the presidency—a sharp contrast to Democratic behavior from the 1930s to the 1960s, when that party enjoyed an advantage in presidential elections. In the 1970s, Congress greatly expanded the size of its committee and subcommittee staffs, thus enabling the House and Senate to monitor and supervise closely the activities of executive agencies. Through the 1974 Budget and Impoundment Act, Congress has sought to increase its control over fiscal policy. Congress has also enacted a number of statutory restrictions on presidential authority in the realm of foreign policy, including the Foreign Commitments Resolution and the Arms Export Control Act.

Finally, congressional investigations, often conducted in conjunction with media exposés and judicial proceedings, have been effective in constraining executive power. Ironically, the techniques that have contributed to the Republican dominance of presidential elections have left them vulnerable to these tactics. The GOP's effective use of television has helped it win presidential elections without engaging in the long and arduous task of building up grassroots electoral organizations. If it possessed strong organizational ties to its supporters, the GOP would not be so vulnerable to investigations and allegations aired through the media.

Institutional combat of the sort that has characterized

17

American politics in recent years is most likely to occur when the major branches of government are controlled by hostile political forces. This condition is neither exclusively nor necessarily associated with divided partisan control of Congress and the presidency.[18] On the one hand, during periods of unified partisan control, institutional combat can occur when hostile factions of the same party are entrenched in different branches of government. For example, right-wing Republicans led by Joseph McCarthy in the early 1950s and antiwar Democrats led by J. William Fulbright in the mid-1960s used legislative investigations to attack presidents belonging to their own parties. On the other hand, divided control is not likely to result in intense institutional struggles in the absence of deep cleavages between the two parties. For example, in the mid- and late 1950s, when moderates and internationalists controlled both the Democratic and Republican parties, relations between the Eisenhower White House and the Rayburn-Johnson Congress were reasonably amicable. However, when divided partisan control of government does coincide with sharp cleavages between the two parties, the importance of institutional conflict relative to electoral competition is likely to increase. This state of affairs has characterized American politics since the Vietnam and Watergate eras.

Deadlock in the electoral arena has encouraged contending political forces to attempt to use not only Congress and the presidency but also the federal judiciary, the national security apparatus, and the mass media as instruments of political combat. These institutions, in turn, have been able to ally with such forces and to bolster their own autonomy and power. Through this process, institutions that are not directly subject to the control of the electorate

18

have become major players in contemporary American politics.

Such institutions were used as instruments of governance and political struggle during earlier periods in the United States. In the decades prior to the 1930s, for example, business interests relied upon the federal courts to check the hostile forces that controlled state legislatures in the Midwest and West. And Progressive reformers, in an effort to circumvent the influence that business exercised through the courts, sponsored the creation of what then was a novel institution, the independent regulatory commission. What is notable about the present period, however, is the extent to which nonelectoral institutions have become central to political struggle in the United States.

The Courts

In the late 1930s and the 1940s an alliance developed between the federal judiciary and liberal political forces. Faced with the threat of Franklin Roosevelt's court-packing plan, the Supreme Court found it prudent to abandon its ties to the conservative camp and to take up such issues as civil rights and civil liberties. Liberals enjoyed access to both Congress and the presidency, but the influence of the South within the New Deal coalition prevented them from relying on these institutions to protect the rights of racial minorities and political dissenters. For this reason they found the federal judiciary an attractive institutional ally. During the 1950s and the 1960s, in response to cases brought by liberal groups, the courts put an end to legally mandated segregation in southern school systems, strengthened First Amendment guarantees, and expanded the rights of persons accused of crimes.[19]

In the 1970s and early 1980s, liberal political forces came to rely even more extensively on judicial power. Lacking access to the White House, they not only sought to expand the range of judicially protected rights but also undertook to use the courts to gain influence in the administrative process. For example, the major environmental statutes enacted by Congress in the 1970s allowed liberal public-interest groups to help shape the implementation of environmental policy through litigation. The federal judiciary found that cooperation with liberal forces helped it to greatly expand its power. Liberals, including important members of Congress, staunchly defended the judiciary against opponents seeking to limit the jurisdiction and enforcement powers of the federal courts.[20]

At the end of the 1980s, however, the addition of three Reagan appointees led to the formation of a conservative majority on the Supreme Court. This new majority turned the Court sharply to the right on issues of civil rights and abortion, and aligned it more closely with the White House in struggles between the president and Congress. It is likely that in the 1990s, conservative political forces will seek to use the courts to accomplish what they are unable to achieve through electoral means—just as liberals had done in the 1960s and 1970s.

The National Security Apparatus

In recent years, conservatives have used the military and national security apparatuses as political weapons. From the

1940s into the 1960s, America's "military industrial complex"—the national security apparatus and economic sectors associated with it—had ties to both the Democratic and Republican parties. There was a bipartisan consensus on the importance of containing the Soviet Union and maintaining a powerful military establishment for this purpose. Presidents and members of Congress—Democrats and Republicans alike—supported high levels of military spending, the construction of new weapons systems, and the vigorous use of American military force abroad. Indeed, if there was any difference between the parties during this period, it was the Democrats who were more consistent advocates of high levels of defense spending. Prior to the Vietnam War, the two largest military buildups of the postwar decades were sponsored by the Democratic administrations of Harry Truman and John F. Kennedy; the Republican administration of Dwight Eisenhower was the most diligent in seeking to economize on defense.[21]

Conflict over the Vietnam War shattered this bipartisan consensus. Opponents of the war came to play a major role in the Democratic party, seeking to challenge the use of American military force abroad and to slash defense spending. Conservative Republicans saw the new Democratic stance on defense issues as a threat to America's security and, at the same time, as an opportunity to expand the GOP's social and political base.

By promoting an enormous military buildup, Republicans have moved to attach to their party political institutions, social forces, and economic interests with a stake in defense programs. The goal of this endeavor is not simply to secure campaign contributions and votes, but more important, to also create a governing apparatus akin to the one the Democrats established during the New Deal and post-war decades. Democratic administrations had used domestic spending programs to solidify the party's ties to its numerous constituency groups. These federal spending programs (as specified by Keynesian theory) in turn stimulated economic growth and employment. While professing to reject the economic theory associated with Democratic spending programs, Republicans have adapted what might be described as "military Keynesianism." Their military programs directly benefit segments of the business community and regions of the country whose fortunes are tied to the military sector. Through military programs, the Republicans seek to achieve economic growth and high levels of employment without limiting the prerogatives of corporate management.

The Media

A third set of institutions whose political importance has increased as a result of party decline and electoral deadlock are the mass media. The media of the nineteenth century were largely subordinate to political parties. Newspapers depended upon official patronage—legal notices and party subsidies—for their financial survival and were controlled by party leaders. At the turn of the century, with the development of commercial advertising, newspapers became financially independent. This made possible the emergence of a formally nonpartisan press.

Presidents were the first national officials to see the opportunities in this development. By communicating directly to the electorate through newspapers and magazines, Theodore Roosevelt and Woodrow Wilson established political constituencies for themselves independent of party organizations and strengthened their own power relative to Congress. President Franklin D. Roosevelt used the radio, most notably in his famous "fireside chats," to reach out to voters throughout the nation and make himself the center of American politics. FDR was also adept at developing close personal relationships with reporters, and these enabled him to obtain favorable news coverage despite the fact that in his day a majority of newspaper owners and publishers were staunch conservatives.[22] Following Roosevelt's example, subsequent presidents sought to use the media to enhance their popularity and power. For example, through televised news conferences, President John F. Kennedy mobilized public support for his domestic and foreign policy initiatives.

The Vietnam War shattered this relationship between the press and the presidency. During the early stages of U.S. involvement, American officials in Vietnam who disapproved of the way the war was being conducted leaked information critical of administration policy to reporters.[23] Publication of this material infuriated Presidents Kennedy and Johnson. On one occasion President Kennedy went so far as to ask the *New York Times* to reassign its Saigon correspondent. The national print and broadcast media—the network news divisions, the national news weeklies, the *Washington Post* and *New York Times*—discovered, however, that there was an audience for critical coverage among segments of the public skeptical of administration policy.[24]

Growing opposition to the war among liberals led members of Congress to break with President Johnson. These shifts in popular and congressional sentiment encouraged

23

journalists and publishers to continue to present critical news reports. Through this process, journalists developed a commitment to "investigative reporting," while a constituency emerged that would rally to the defense of the media when they came under White House attack.

The electoral deadlock and attendant conflicts between president and Congress in the 1970s and 1980s further strengthened the media's role in political struggles. Opponents of the Nixon and Reagan administrations welcomed news accounts critical of the conduct of executive agencies and officials. At the same time, by conducting televised hearings, members of Congress found it possible to mobilize national constituencies against the administration.

For their part, the national media were able to enhance their autonomy and carve out a prominent place for themselves in American government and politics by aggressively investigating, publicizing, and exposing instances of official misconduct.[25] Conservative forces during the Nixon and Reagan years responded to media criticism by denouncing the press as biased and seeking to curb it. However, members of Congress and groups opposed to presidential policies have benefited from the growing influence of the press and have been prepared to defend it when it comes under attack. For example, in the 1970s, this constituency excoriated efforts by the Nixon White House to block publication of the Pentagon Papers. In the 1980s, the same forces denounced, as an illegitimate effort to chill free speech and undermine the First Amendment, the conservative-financed libel suit brought by General William Westmoreland against CBS. The emergence of these overlapping interests, more than any ideological bias, explains why the national news media seem so often to be aligned with liberal political forces against the White House.

While the influence of the media in national politics has increased, the decay of party organizations has made politicians ever more dependent upon favorable media coverage. National political leaders and journalists have had symbiotic relationships at least since FDR's presidency, but initially politicians were the senior partners. They benefited from media publicity but were not totally dependent upon it as long as they could still rely upon party organizations to mobilize votes. Journalists, on the other hand, depended upon their relationships with politicians for access to information, and they would hesitate to report stories that might antagonize valuable sources. For example, reporters did not publicize potentially embarrassing information, widely known in Washington, about the personal lives of such figures as Franklin D. Roosevelt and John F. Kennedy.

With the decline of party, the balance of power between politicians and journalists has been reversed. Now that politicians have become heavily dependent upon the media to reach their constituents, journalists no longer need fear that their access to information can be restricted in retaliation for negative coverage. In contrast to journalistic silence in the early 1960s regarding President Kennedy's marital infidelity, the news media in 1988 and 1989 showed no hesitation in revealing Gary Hart's extramarital affairs and Representative Barney Frank's sexual indiscretions.

After 1980, Republican presidents reacted to these developments by fashioning new techniques of media management. FDR had circumvented hostile newspaper pub-

25

lishers by establishing direct ties to reporters. Ronald Reagan sought to circumvent what he perceived to be unfriendly journalists by reaching the public directly through the television camera. His advisers curtailed reporters' access to the president by drastically reducing the number of presidential press conferences and other opportunities for reporters to question Reagan directly. His advisers also undertook to harness the media to their own political purposes by creating events filled with patriotic symbols and appeals that the media were able neither to attack nor ignore. The spectacle created to accompany the unveiling of the refurbished Statue of Liberty is a case in point. The 1988 Bush campaign sought to make use of these same media techniques. However, Reagan and Bush were not able to prevent their opponents from using damaging media revelations to attack their administrations. These revelations are a central component of what has become one of the most important weapons of contemporary political warfare—revelation, investigation, and prosecution.

REVELATION, INVESTIGATION, PROSECUTION

The strengthening of the national news media and the federal judiciary has given rise to a major new technique of political combat—revelation, investigation, and prosecution. The acronym for this, RIP, is a fitting political epitaph for the public officials who have become its targets. The RIP weaponry was initially forged by opponents of the Nixon administration in their struggles with the White House, and through the Reagan years it was used primarily by congressional Democrats to attack their foes in the executive branch. More recently, however, Republicans have also begun to wield the RIP weapon.

After his reelection in 1972, President Nixon undertook to expand executive power at the expense of Congress by impounding appropriated funds and reorganizing executive agencies without legislative authorization.[26] In addition, the White House established the "plumbers" squad to plug leaks of information to Congress and the press, and (its opponents claimed) it sought to undermine the legitimacy of the federal judiciary by appointing unqualified justices to the Supreme Court. The administration's adversaries also claimed that it sought to limit Congress's influence over foreign policy by keeping vital information from it, most notably in the "secret bombing" of Cambodia.

At the same time, Nixon sought to curtail the influence of the national news media. His administration brought suit against the *New York Times* in an effort to block publication of the Pentagon Papers and threatened, under the rubric of promoting ideological diversity, to compel the national television networks to sell the local stations they owned. The president's opponents declared the administration's actions to be abuses of power, and these efforts animated their attack upon Richard Nixon in the Watergate controversy.

The attack began with a series of revelations in the *Washington Post* linking the White House to a break-in at the Watergate headquarters of the Democratic National Committee. The *Post*'s reporters were quickly joined by scores of investigative journalists from the *New York Times, Newsweek, Time* magazine, and the television networks.

As revelations of misdeeds by the Nixon White House proliferated, the administration's opponents in Congress demanded a full legislative investigation. In response, the Senate created a special committee, chaired by Senator Sam Ervin, to investigate White House misconduct in the 1972 presidential election. Investigators for the Ervin committee uncovered numerous questionable activities on the part of Nixon's aides, and these were revealed to the public during a series of dramatic, nationally televised hearings.

Evidence of criminal activity unearthed by the Ervin committee led to congressional pressure for the appointment of a special prosecutor. Ultimately, a large number of high-ranking administration officials were indicted, convicted, and imprisoned. Impeachment proceedings were initiated against President Nixon himself, and when evidence was found linking Nixon directly to the cover-up of the Watergate burglary, he was compelled to resign from office. Thus, with the help of the RIP weaponry, the Nixon administration's antagonists were able to achieve a total victory in their conflict with the president. Although no subsequent president has been driven from office, opponents of presidential administrations have since used the RIP process to attack and weaken their foes in the executive branch.

The RIP process became institutionalized when Congress adopted the 1978 Ethics in Government Act, which established procedures facilitating the appointment of special prosecutors to deal with allegations of wrongdoing in the executive branch. The act also defined as criminal several forms of influence peddling in which executive officials had traditionally engaged, such as lobbying former associates after leaving office. (Such activities are also traditional on Capitol Hill, but Congress chose not to impose the restrictions embodied in the act upon its own members and staff.)

In this way, Congress defined new crimes that executive branch officials could be charged with committing.

The extent to which the RIP process has come to be a routine facet of American politics became evident during the Iran-contra conflict. After the diversion of funds to the contras was revealed, it was universally assumed that Congress should conduct televised hearings and the judiciary appoint an independent counsel to investigate the officials involved in the episode. Yet this procedure is really quite remarkable: Officials who in other democracies would merely be compelled to resign from office are threatened with criminal prosecution in the United States. Subsequently, Republicans made use of Congress's own ethics code and the Ethics Committee to launch their successful attacks upon the House Democratic leadership.

As a result of these developments, revelations and investigations of misconduct by public figures have become a major vehicle of political competition in the United States. The central means through which liberal political forces attacked the White House and mobilized support for themselves during the Reagan administration were investigations of EPA administrator Ann Burford Gorsuch, Attorney General Edwin Meese, and Supreme Court nominee Robert Bork, as well as hearings on the Iran-contra affair.

During the early months of the Bush presidency, partisan warfare chiefly took the form of allegations of misconduct that Democrats and Republicans lodged against one another. Senate Democrats were able to defeat John Tower's confirmation as secretary of defense with charges that his record of alcohol abuse, sexual impropriety, and ties to defense contractors rendered him unfit to head the Defense

Department. Republicans then drove Democratic House Speaker Wright from office with accusations of financial misdeeds, including allegations that Wright and his wife received large sums of money from a real estate developer and used inflated royalties from a book contract as a cover for exceeding limits in congressional rules on outside income. At roughly the same time, charges of improper loans and investments compelled Democratic House Whip Tony Coelho to resign. Congressional Democrats responded with allegations that Wright's chief accuser, Republican House Whip Newt Gingrich, also reaped improper profits from a book contract and was involved in dubious campaign fundraising activities. Subsequently, House Democrats launched an investigation of Republican manipulation of the Department of Housing and Urban Development under former secretary Samuel Pierce. Later, House Republicans called upon Democratic Representative Barney Frank to resign after embarrassing accounts of his personal life appeared in the press.

Three trends in contemporary American politics have led to the emergence of RIP as a central vehicle of political competition in the United States: growing electoral deadlock, the decline of party organizations, and the increasing power of the mass media. Unable to gain control of their opponents' institutional bastion through the normal channels of electoral competition, Democrats and Republicans have learned to use allegations of impropriety to discredit and weaken one another. Public officials have become increasingly vulnerable to such attacks as party organizations have declined. In contemporary America, journalists have supplanted party leaders as the public's most important source of information and opinion concerning elected officials, so that when information critical of an official dominates media coverage, that official's public support quickly evaporates. The willingness of the press to ferret out and disclose damaging information about public officials, more than the pursuit of a partisan or ideological agenda, reflects the increasing power of the media in American politics. For example, the *Washington Post* and the *New York Times* investigated the business dealings of Democrat Jim Wright as aggressively as those of Republican Ed Meese.

POSTELECTORAL POLITICS AND GOVERNMENTAL DISARRAY

America has now entered an era in which institutional combat has increased in importance relative to electoral competition. This is not to say that electoral outcomes can make no difference. If the Republicans were able to break the Democratic stranglehold on Congress or the Democrats were able more than occasionally to overcome the GOP's advantage in the presidential arena, the stalemate that has characterized American electoral politics for the past quarter century would be broken and the patterns of institutional combat we describe would become less prominent.

Elections can have an impact even under present conditions. In 1980, the Republican capture of the White House and Senate and the party's unusually strong gains in House races enabled Ronald Reagan to secure the enactment of major changes in tax and budget policy. President Reagan's dominance of American government lasted for little more than a year, however, before the momentum of the "Reagan Revolution" was broken by institutional struggles, as discussed in subsequent chapters.

The one election in the past two decades that gave a single party control over the presidency and both houses of Congress—the election of 1976—had little effect on prevailing patterns of American government. Though a member of their party occupied the White House, congressional Democrats had acquired such a stake in legislative power and had so little confidence in their ability to maintain control of the presidency that they refused to follow Jimmy Carter's leadership and continued their attack on presidential power. More than a short-term break in the contemporary electoral deadlock—which has endured for nearly a generation—would be required to shift the focus of American politics from institutional combat back to the electoral arena.

Governmental Disarray

The postelectoral political order that has emerged in the United States has three consequences that, taken together, contribute to the disarray of American government and pose problems for the nation's place in the world. First, as each party has strengthened the institutions it commands, the constitutional separation of powers has been transformed into a system of dual sovereignty. The Democrats have undertaken to endow Congress and allied institutions with administrative and coercive capacities that give them the power to govern without controlling the executive branch. In a parallel fashion, the Republicans have worked to make the presidency an institution capable of governing on its own. As a result, the United States often pursues two divergent and contradictory policy agendas. For example, the White House has supplied and armed contra forces attempting to overthrow the Sandinista regime in Nicaragua. When Congress would not appropriate money for this purpose and prohibited American intelligence agencies from distributing arms and supplies to the Contras, the White House established its own funding and supply network. Congressional Democrats, for their part, have pursued an independent Central American policy and, under the leadership of former House Speaker Jim Wright, conducted their own negotiations with the Sandinista regime.

Second, the American governmental system is increasingly characterized by the absence of political closure. Electoral stalemate and the enhanced political power of non-electoral institutions means that the question of who will govern—and, equally important, who will *not* govern—is less likely to be resolved in the electoral arena. Because the "winners" in the electoral process do not acquire firm control of the government and the "losers" are not deprived of power, governments are characteristically too weak to implement policies that impose costs upon powerful political interests. This political weakness often compels politicians to pay greater heed to the implications of policies for domestic political struggles than their implications for collective national purposes. For example, Republican presidents have tolerated enormous budget deficits despite the dangers they pose to the nation's economy because these deficits provide them with a way of undercutting Democratic social programs that they have not been strong enough to attack directly.[27]

33

Third, the political patterns emerging in the United States are undermining the administrative capabilities of the American state. As Congress and the president struggle to gain control of segments of the state apparatus, administrative agencies become battlegrounds and can be rendered incapable of carrying out their governmental tasks. During such conflict, bureaucrats opposed to administration policy typically leak to Congress and the media information that can damage their superiors, officials fearing investigation retain legal counsel, and in short order, the operations of the agency grind to a halt. For example, during Ronald Reagan's first term in office, the work of the Environmental Protection Agency (EPA) was seriously disrupted as the administration undertook to reorient the agency's approach to the enforcement of environmental policy and the president's opponents in Congress sought to prevent him from doing so.[28]

Struggles between Congress and the president also provide subordinate officials in the executive branch with the opportunity to increase their autonomy. Officials seeking to pursue an independent course can use the media to generate support in Congress, thereby preventing their superiors from reining them in. A master of this technique during the Reagan years was Rudolph Giuliani, the U.S. attorney in New York. Giuliani brought indictments against Ferdinand and Imelda Marcos, though this ran counter to the administration's policy of granting asylum to dictators so as to encourage them to relinquish power. Any effort by the administration to prevent the Marcos indictments would have caused an enormous furor in the press and precipitated a hostile congressional investigation. Similar considerations enabled the U.S. attorney in Miami to bring an indictment against Panamanian strongman Manuel Noriega, leaving him no choice but to hold onto power to avoid being extradited to the United States. Thus the administrative capabilities of the American state have been disrupted to the point where subordinate officials in the Department of Justice are able to alter the course of the nation's foreign policy.

Underlying America's current governmental disarray is the decay of electoral democracy in the United States. The electoral deadlock which helped to produce contemporary patterns of political struggle, as we have noted, emerged from the destruction of the nation's traditional electoral institutions, in particular from the collapse of political party organizations and the concomitant erosion of voter turnout to the point where, at most, 50 percent of the eligible electorate goes to the polls. Today, rather than focus on outmobilizing their opponents in the electoral arena, political leaders increasingly employ institutional weapons of political struggle that neither require nor encourage popular mobilization. Through such techniques as RIP, political actors with a narrow base of popular support (e.g., journalists, federal prosecutors, and public-interest groups) can end the careers of politicians such as presidents and big-city mayors, who enjoy a broader popular base. And when political struggle takes this form, voters are given little reason to participate. Thus the contemporary system of institutional combat emerged from and helps to perpetuate a political order characterized by remarkably limited popular mobilization.

This postelectoral pattern has become increasingly entrenched in recent years because it serves the interests of major political actors. Political forces lacking a broad popular base obviously benefit from forms of competition that do not allocate power in proportion to mass support. Elected officials and party politicians also have reason to be satisfied with the present state of affairs. The constricted electorate helps to maintain the Republicans' hold on the presidency. The Democrats have established an even firmer grip on Congress and have been able to strengthen it as an instrument of both governance and political combat.

Neither party is prepared to assume the risks that seeking to change the present system would entail. To break the electoral deadlock underlying this system, large numbers of new voters would have to be brought into the electorate— and each party fears that a significant expansion of the electorate would threaten its hold on the institution it currently controls. Postelectoral political patterns and the governmental consequences that flow from them have thus become deeply entrenched features of the contemporary American political order.

2

Electoral Deadlock

THE PRESENT DEMOCRATIC AND REPUBLICAN coalitions emerged from the turmoil of the 1960s. From the 1930s through the 1960s, America had been governed by a regime whose foundations were laid by Franklin D. Roosevelt. But the political alliances that characterized the New Deal system were shattered by a series of struggles sparked by the Vietnam War, the civil rights movement, and the decline of America's international economic competitiveness.

Two major efforts to create a successor to the New Deal system emerged from the disarray of the 1960s. The first, associated most prominently with Ronald Reagan, was an attempt to join together business, social conservatives, and middle-income taxpayers in a reconstituted Republican coalition of the political right, organized around a revitalized private sector and a national security state. The second was an effort to use the resources and powers of the domestic state to unify organized labor, blacks, public employees, and middle-class liberal activists in a post–New Deal Democratic coalition.

Clashes between and within the reconstituted right and

post–New Deal liberal political coalitions have resulted in electoral deadlock in the United States since the 1960s— deadlock stemming from Republican dominance of presidential elections and Democratic primacy in congressional races.

THE COLLAPSE OF AMERICA'S POSTWAR REGIME

American government during the two decades following World War II rested on a remarkably broad social base. The New Deal coalition that Franklin D. Roosevelt constructed in the 1930s drew its votes from southerners, unionized workers, urban ethnics, northern blacks, and middle-class liberals. Most members of the business community opposed New Deal labor and social legislation, but after World War II the Democrats reached an accommodation with many of their former opponents.[1] Industrialists were reconciled to the New Deal because the wartime destruction of the European and Japanese economies enabled American firms to dominate world markets, and Keynesian fiscal policies and social spending programs contributed to unprecedented prosperity at home. Manufacturers in defense industries supported America's postwar governing coalition because the nation's rearmament during the Truman administration brought them healthy profits.[2]

Conditions of Regime Stability

The stability of America's postwar regime depended on three conditions that characterized the national and international political economies during the two decades that followed World War II. The first condition was that the costs of building and maintaining the system of international alliances and protectorates that the United States constructed must not undermine domestic political support for a foreign policy of internationalism. One of these costs was economic. The permanent military establishment that America maintained during the Cold War years had to be financed by some combination of taxation, government borrowing, and inflation; but as long as the economy grew at a reasonable rate—which it did, for the most part, throughout the postwar period—the burdens this imposed upon the electorate were not onerous. Another cost of empire was conscription, but to the extent that children of the middle and upper classes could avoid military service through student deferments, the draft did not threaten the most politically influential segments of the population.

The second condition for the survival of America's postwar government was that American industry retain its competitiveness in world markets. Financial and commercial interests with a stake in international trade could exist in political coalition with the employees and owners of industrial firms only if the trade policies promoted by the former group did not cost the latter their jobs or profits. In addition, to win the support of labor, agriculture, middle-class liberals, and the beneficiaries of social entitlement programs, the postwar governing coalition relied on a policy of universal payoffs or, in Theodore Lowi's terminology, "interest-group liberalism."[3] This was a costly strategy. Politicians who practiced it could retain the acquiescence of these interest-group members in their capacity as taxpayers and consumers only if the economy grew at a sufficient pace to enable Washington to avoid higher tax rates and highly inflationary fiscal and monetary policies. In the international system of free trade promoted by the United States during the postwar period, this economic growth depended on the ability of American firms to compete successfully with foreign firms in both domestic and overseas markets.

Third, a coalition composed both of southern whites and northern blacks and liberals could endure only as long as the issue of race was submerged. Roosevelt had succeeded in keeping it that way during his presidency, but Democratic party and congressional leaders found it an increasingly difficult issue to manage during the late 1940s and the 1950s.[4]

Breakdown of the Postwar Regime

During the 1960s and 1970s, changes in the national and international political and economic systems (which were brought about, in part, by policies intended to stabilize America's postwar governing coalition) violated these three conditions and ultimately shattered the nation's governing coalition. Conflicts over race, the Vietnam War, and the fiscal and regulatory policies of the national government were political manifestations of these changes.

Race-related issues were the first to emerge. Postwar agricultural policies stimulated the mechanization, consolidation, and internationalization of American agriculture, driving millions of black sharecroppers from the rural South to northern cities. To win their votes, northern Democrats took up the cause of civil rights for blacks in the

South.[5] In addition, Washington's efforts in the 1960s to expand American influence in the Third World, where the British and French empires had recently disintegrated, were damaged by the system of racial segregation in the South. This threat to U.S. interests gave presidents John F. Kennedy and Lyndon B. Johnson another reason to bring the federal government into the campaign for black civil rights. Their actions led many southern whites to abandon the Democratic party in presidential elections—the first major element of the New Deal coalition to do so.[6]

As long as the crusade for civil rights was confined to the South, it enjoyed widespread support among all elements of the Democratic coalition in the North. That state of affairs was short-lived. The sight of their brothers and sisters rising up against oppressive conditions in the South encouraged blacks in northern cities to do the same. The political mobilization of blacks enabled northern liberals to increase their influence relative to other elements of the Democratic coalition—urban machine politicians, labor leaders, and working-class and lower-middle-class ethnics.

The alliance between upper-middle-class liberals and blacks was consummated through the various urban programs of the New Frontier and Great Society. These programs provided federal funds to finance "innovative" programs that would help the "culturally disadvantaged" in inner-city neighborhoods—circumventing local governments and municipal bureaucracies, which were castigated for being "insensitive" and unresponsive to the needs of the "community."[7] The working-class and lower-middle-class ethnics who controlled and staffed municipal governments and bureaucracies in most northern cities fully under-

41

stood that these euphemisms signalled the redistribution of public benefits at their expense. Many of these voters therefore turned against Democratic presidential candidates.

Opposition to the Johnson administration's policies in Southeast Asia generated the second major split in America's postwar governing coalition. The Vietnam War was a logical consequence of the nation's postwar foreign policy: Wars and indigenous uprisings are natural concomitants of empire building. The United States had fought just such a war in Korea in the early 1950s. The Korean War had not been especially popular at home, but public unease with it never escalated into active resistance and disruption.[8] What helped turn the intense but initially limited opposition to America's involvement in Vietnam into one of the largest and most disruptive mass movements in American history was a shift in the Johnson administration's conscription policies.

Precisely because Johnson was committed to civil rights, he was embarrassed by the charge that a disproportionate number of American soldiers and war casualties in Vietnam were black. In seeking to be fair, the Johnson administration limited college-student deferments and thus helped create an antiwar constituency that included a substantial segment of the middle class—students (and the parents of students) at universities such as Kent State and Colorado State, not just Berkeley and Harvard. To avoid further undermining domestic political support for his administration, President Johnson hesitated to raise taxes to finance the war. This boosted the rate of inflation, further weakening middle-class support for the Democrats.

The erosion of America's dominant position in the world economy also contributed to the collapse of the nation's postwar governing coalition. Again, policies pursued by Washington contributed to this development. The United States had helped its allies in Europe and Japan rebuild their economies after World War II—most notably through the Marshall Plan—to strengthen their resistance to Soviet military pressure and to prevent local communist parties from gaining internal influence.[9] By so doing, Washington helped create the very competitors that later challenged the preeminent position of American firms in many world markets. By assuming the role of defender of the free world, the United States also saddled its economy with military costs that were proportionately greater than those borne by its trading partners.

More recently, the 1973 price increase by the Organization of Petroleum Exporting Countries (OPEC)—and the decade of inflation and economic stagnation it precipitated—further weakened the U.S. economy. American firms producing new products were hard pressed to absorb workers who had lost their jobs in industries that no longer were able to compete with foreign manufacturers. The OPEC increase was also partly a consequence of American national security policy. The Nixon administration had indicated to OPEC that it would tolerate a steep price increase because the revenues generated would enable the shah of Iran to finance weapons purchases and police the Persian Gulf—a role that the administration wanted him to play but that Congress was unwilling to underwrite.[10]

The difficulties that the American economy experienced in the 1970s placed great strains on the postwar coalition. Both workers and industrialists in sectors of the economy that were no longer internationally competitive abandoned their prior commitment to a central tenet of that coalition—

free trade. Many middle-class taxpayers and members of the business community no longer believed that they, their firms, or the nation as a whole could afford to fight a war on poverty—a conviction whose most dramatic expression was the tax-revolt movement of the late 1970s.

BUILDING A NEW POLITICAL ORDER

Against the backdrop of these political upheavals, a number of political leaders and groups sought to reshape politics and government in the United States. On the liberal end of the political spectrum, several movements emerged espousing such causes as consumerism, environmentalism, and feminism. These movements have often been called the forces of the "new politics," to distinguish them from the labor leaders, white southerners, and other old-line politicians with whom they competed for influence within the Democratic party. On the other side of the ideological spectrum, Republican politicians and conservative political activists sought to mobilize disgruntled taxpayers, the religious right, and members of the business community.

The Post-1960s Democrats

The liberal political movements that challenged the New Deal system were spearheaded by young members of the upper middle class. For them, the struggle against racial segregation and the Vietnam War were formative experiences, just as the Great Depression and World War II had been for their parents. The antiwar and civil rights movements led these young men and women to define themselves as a political force in opposition to the public policies, political actors, and governmental institutions of the nation's postwar regime.

In the late 1960s and early 1970s, liberal movements were remarkably successful in securing the enactment of policies they favored and in undermining the power and prerogatives of the postwar governing coalition. Opponents of the Vietnam War ultimately forced the withdrawal of American forces from Southeast Asia. Through the War Powers Act, the Foreign Commitments Resolution, the Arms Export Control Act, and stricter scrutiny of the Central Intelligence Agency (CIA), liberal activists also imposed some limits on the president's ability to use American troops, intelligence operatives, and weapons to prop up anticommunist regimes abroad. Thus, a central thrust of American foreign policy during the Cold War was restrained, although not entirely reversed.

Liberal activists also played a major role in securing the enactment of environmental, consumer, and occupational health and safety legislation that significantly restricted the prerogatives of business managers. These statutes not only imposed limits on the goods business firms could produce and the ways they could produce them but also required firms to invest capital in equipment that would promote a cleaner environment and safer products and working conditions.[11] In addition, environmental and community activists defeated numerous public works projects that had been designed to channel public resources to coalitions of local officials, business interests, and construction unions. And antinuclear activists largely brought the billion-dollar nuclear power industry to its knees.

In recent years these same political forces have secured the enactment of bottle-return and antismoking regulations that seek to restrict—and stigmatize—the behavior of the working and lower middle classes, much as the Prohibition movement did. And despite the failure of the campaign to ratify the Equal Rights Amendment, feminists have enjoyed considerable success in the congressional arena. For example, they won the passage of legislation, opposed by the insurance industry, that increased the pension benefits of women, and they have gained some official recognition for the principle of equal pay for jobs of "comparable worth."

Liberal activists also successfully attacked the political institutions and procedures upon which the power of their opponents rested. The best-known example is the McGovern-Fraser Commission, which changed the Democratic party's presidential nomination procedures in ways that reduced the influence of the party's traditional power brokers.[12] In addition, the environmental and consumer movements (which command considerable legal talent) drafted regulatory legislation that provided manifold opportunities for public-interest law firms to sue executive officials who were not enforcing these laws to their satisfaction. And organizations such as Common Cause pressed for the enactment of the Freedom of Information Act and various sunshine laws that would enable them to best use their access to the mass media.

A second force that mobilized against the established leadership of the Democratic party was the white South. During the 1960s, southern whites fought in a variety of ways against the civil rights policies of the national Democratic regime and the growing influence of liberals in the Democratic party's affairs. Southern senators filibustered against civil rights legislation, southern state governments adopted a posture of massive resistance to desegregation, and some southerners resorted to violence against civil rights workers. In 1968, George Wallace's independent presidential candidacy galvanized southern voters and led millions to desert the Democratic ticket. Since that time, many southern whites have supported Republican presidential candidates even as they voted for Democrats in congressional and local races.

Blacks, a third element of the Democratic coalition, have sought in recent decades to play a larger role in American politics. During the 1960s, the civil rights movement, the federal courts, and the programs of Lyndon Johnson's Great Society provided blacks with new channels of political influence. The 1965 Voting Rights Act enfranchised millions of new black voters, but it was not until Jesse Jackson's presidential candidacies in 1984 and 1988 that blacks played a major independent role in Democratic nominating politics.

In the face of these challenges, labor leaders and established party politicians have struggled to maintain their influence. Labor unions stepped up their lobbying and electoral efforts during the 1970s and 1980s. In the 1980s, Democratic moderates and conservatives organized the Democratic Leadership Council in an effort to reassert their position in party affairs.

The Reconstituted Right

The victories that the liberal political forces achieved through Congress and the courts helped alienate a number

47

of political groups, including business leaders, southern whites, and segments of the middle class. These groups, which formerly had supported the nation's postwar governing coalition, joined together to form what can be called the "reconstituted right." First, industrialists whose firms were unable to compete successfully in world markets attributed many of their problems to recently implemented regulatory policies that had increased their production costs and to burgeoning social welfare expenditures that directly or indirectly had increased their labor costs. Even businessmen in sectors of the economy that remained internationally competitive had reason to oppose these regulatory and social expenditure policies, on the grounds that they contributed to inflation.

In the 1970s, a number of business leaders worked to politically revitalize the nation's corporate community. This revitalization was expressed through (1) the organization of the Business Roundtable, which successfully fought both the efforts of consumer groups to establish a consumer protection agency and those of the American Federation of Labor (AFL) to reform the nation's labor laws; (2) the increased willingness of businessmen to finance institutions—such as the American Enterprise Institute and the Heritage Foundation—that propounded the principles of free enterprise; and (3) the phenomenal growth in the late 1970s of business political action committees (PACs).[13]

The Democratic party also suffered massive defections during the 1960s and 1970s because of its identification with racial minorities and various liberal movements.[14] In presidential elections after 1960, as figure 2.1 indicates, a

FIGURE 2.1
DECLINING SUPPORT FOR DEMOCRATIC
PRESIDENTIAL CANDIDATES AMONG
SOUTHERN WHITES, 1964–1984

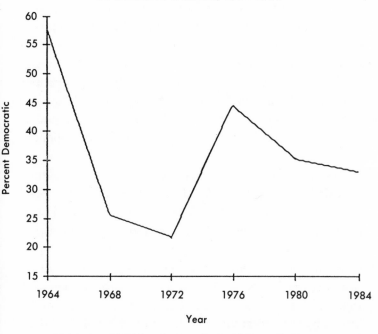

SOURCE: University of Michigan Institute for Social Research. Data were made available through the Inter-University Consortium for Political and Social Research.

substantial proportion of the southern white electorate abandoned the Democrats. Many southerners as well as many Catholics and evangelical Protestants from other regions of the country were deeply offended by the stances of national Democratic politicians on abortion, school prayer, gay rights, and other social issues.

49

During the 1970s, the erosion of America's status in the world economy, coupled with accelerating domestic inflation in the aftermath of the Vietnam War, threatened the economic position of large segments of America's middle class. Many voters who previously had been willing to tolerate social-welfare spending (and the taxes needed to support it) now became open to the appeals of politicians advocating tax reduction. The dramatic success of Proposition 13 in California indicated the potential of this issue and encouraged Republicans to exploit the Democratic party's identification with high levels of social spending and taxation.

Finally, a striking regional division became evident in American electoral politics during the 1970s. Voters in regions of the country least affected by the declining competitiveness of American heavy industry—that is, the South and the West—not surprisingly found the case for a free market economy more persuasive than did their counterparts in the midwestern and northeastern industrial belt. This made them likely prospects for mobilization by conservative opponents of the regulatory and social welfare programs enacted by the Democrats.[15] These voters, along with those unhappy with the Democratic party's positions on racial and social issues, provided the Republicans with their margins of victory in presidential elections between 1968 and 1988. All but three western states cast their electoral votes for the GOP candidate in every one of the last six presidential elections (see figure 2.2). The states of the South were strongly Republican in four of these six elections, but they twice supported regional candidates: George Wallace in 1968 and Jimmy Carter in 1976.

FIGURE 2.2
WESTERN SUPPORT FOR REPUBLICAN PRESIDENTIAL
CANDIDATES, 1968–1988

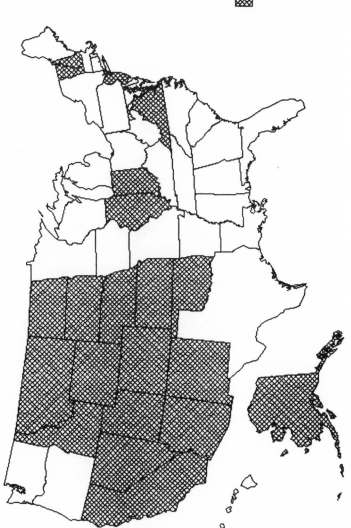

 States carried by
the Republicans in
all presidential
races, 1968–1988.

PRESIDENTIAL ELECTIONS:
THE DEMOCRATS

Over the past twenty years, Democratic contenders for the White House have sought in a variety of ways to construct political coalitions that would allow them to secure their party's presidential nomination and to win the general election.

1968: Division and Defeat

In 1968, the leadership of the Democratic party was challenged from two directions. On one side, George Wallace's third-party presidential campaign drew upon southern and working-class white disaffection from the Democratic party on issues of race. On the other side, antiwar activists supported Senator Eugene McCarthy's candidacy for the Democratic nomination. The forces led by McCarthy made no real effort to forge alliances with other elements of the Democratic constituency, but they nevertheless proved powerful enough to dissuade President Johnson from seeking renomination. When Johnson withdrew from the race, established party leaders threw their support to Vice President Hubert Humphrey. At this point, Robert F. Kennedy entered the contest for the Democratic presidential nomination. Kennedy's candidacy attracted party regulars, unionized workers, blacks, and liberals; therefore he hoped to reunite the old Democratic coalition. After Kennedy's assassination, Humphrey secured the nomination; any chance of reuniting the party was shattered during the violent confrontation between the police and antiwar protesters at the Democratic national convention in Chicago.

In the aftermath of the convention, Humphrey found it difficult to rebuild the Democratic coalition. Defeat in the general election persuaded many Democratic leaders that it was necessary to attract liberals back into the party. Toward this end, the Democratic National Committee established the McGovern-Fraser Commission to reform the party's candidate selection procedures in ways favored by the party's liberal wing.

1972: Zenith of the New Politics

Prior to the 1972 election, the McGovern-Fraser Commission rewrote the rules of the Democratic presidential nominating process in two ways that worked to the advantage of liberal activists. The revised process encouraged state parties to select delegates to national party conventions in ways—open caucuses and proportional representation primaries—that increased the weight of middle-class activists in the nominating process. The commission also established delegate quotas that increased the number of women, racial minorities, and young people at the party convention. The quotas gave more weight in the nominating process to groups whose support liberals hoped to cultivate and allowed state delegations headed by party regulars, such as Mayor Richard J. Daley of Chicago, to be unseated on the grounds that they were unrepresentative. These rule changes helped to bring about the nomination of George McGovern, an antiwar Democrat who, not coincidentally, chaired the party committee that rewrote the rules.[16]

In the 1972 presidential election, McGovern was decisively defeated by Richard M. Nixon. Three sources of this defeat merit examination. First, the McGovern candidacy drove large numbers of blue-collar and southern voters out of the Democratic ranks because they feared that they alone would bear the costs of such liberal goals as redressing racial injustice and scaling back the nation's defense commitments. This conflict of interest was exacerbated by the disdain—verging on class hatred—often exhibited by upper-middle-class McGovernites toward members of the working class. Second, McGovern's advocacy of programs that would redistribute income was not well received by middle-class taxpayers, who were beginning to feel the economic effects of inflation induced by the Vietnam War. Third, the McGovern candidacy generated little enthusiasm among blacks, who perceived that it was oriented mainly to the political concerns of a segment of the white upper middle class. The overwhelming majority of blacks who voted in 1972 voted for McGovern, but blacks did not turn out in the numbers anticipated by Democratic strategists.

Among the lessons Democrats drew from the 1972 debacle was that the arena of presidential elections was not the political battleground necessarily most congenial to their fortunes. Many Democratic activists concluded that the executive branch, which formerly had been regarded as the commanding height of the American political terrain, might not in the immediate future be accessible to them. Of course, the Democrats did not cease participating in presidential races, but they began to concentrate their efforts more heavily in other areas of American politics, including Congress and the courts.

1976: A Hollow Victory

Jimmy Carter was able to secure the 1976 Democratic presidential nomination because he was not too closely identified with any faction of the party. The 1972 defeat had convinced many Democrats that to win the presidency, they must recapture the support of those voters who had been alienated by McGovern's links to the party's left wing. As a southerner, Carter was able to attract support below the Mason-Dixon Line, and as an ideological moderate he was acceptable to blue-collar Democrats. At the same time, Carter's civil rights record drew black support, and this legitimated his candidacy in the eyes of white liberals. Though Carter generated very little enthusiasm, the Democrats were able to eke out a narrow victory in the 1976 presidential election. Gerald Ford, the Republican candidate, was if anything weaker, and the GOP had still not recovered from the damage of the Watergate scandal.

Carter's chief virtue as a candidate—namely, that he had no firm political base—proved to be a severe handicap when he assumed office. Virtually every effort Carter made to build a political constituency—by supporting policies attractive to any faction of the Democratic coalition—offended rival factions. Consequently, Carter found it impossible to unite a legislative coalition capable of enacting his major proposals. This political dilemma helped to create the appearance of ineptitude that characterized the Carter administration. At the end of his term, faced with double-digit inflation, the Soviet invasion of Afghanistan, and the Iranian hostage crisis, Carter undertook to cut expenditures on social programs and increase military spending. These policy changes infuriated liberals and some elements of organized labor, who then turned on Carter and sought to block his renomination.

The 1980 Election: Factional Division

In 1980, two major elements of the Democratic coalition—organized labor and liberals—abandoned Carter. Organized labor opposed Carter's renomination and supported Senator Edward Kennedy. Unhappy with both Carter and Kennedy, many liberals supported John Anderson, an obscure Republican representative from Illinois, who ran as an independent presidential candidate in 1980. Anderson had one special attraction: He told audiences what they neither expected nor wanted to hear. For example, he lectured a National Rifle Association convention on the merits of gun control. In the pretelevision era, Anderson would have received scant attention. But in the age of the electronic media, Anderson's "difference" made him news. Virtually overnight, he moved from obscurity to celebrity.

While organized labor and liberals were abandoning Carter because he had cut domestic social programs, many middle-class voters, stung by inflation, were attracted to the Republican presidential candidate Ronald Reagan's proposals for major tax cuts. At the same time, Carter's modest defense buildup did not go far enough to mollify conservative Democrats. Carter's loss of support on both the political left and right enabled Reagan to win the presidential election by a convincing margin.

1984: Reunification and Defeat

During his first term in office, President Reagan slashed taxes and launched assaults on programs central to the interests of organized labor, liberals, and blacks. In 1984, the Democratic presidential candidate Walter F. Mondale sought to unite these three core elements of the Democratic coalition—an effort facilitated by their common desperation in the face of Reaganism. To avoid the danger that these groups would each rally behind a different candidate, Mondale actively solicited early public endorsements from major organizations within each group.[17] He also proposed programs that could link the interests of different segments of his constituency. For example, Mondale endorsed a concept—industrial policy—that, while masquerading as an economic doctrine, was actually a political compact among labor, liberals, and blacks. Industrial policy has many variants, but the version promoted by Mondale called on the federal government to supervise what was said to be the inevitable transformation of the American industrial base from obsolescent smokestack industries to the high technology industries of the future. Government intervention was considered essential for minimizing the human and social costs that otherwise would accompany massive changes in employment and investment.

Industrial policy can be viewed politically as a compact between middle-class liberal activists (who would gain influence over the allocation of capital) and organized labor

57

(whose members were promised job retraining for the high-technology industries of the future). These promises were accompanied by a commitment to repair the nation's infrastructure of roads, bridges, railways, and the like—the 1984 equivalent of New Deal public works programs for displaced workers. Whatever its economic validity, as a political doctrine, industrial policy made a good deal of sense. With the support of organized labor and liberals—as well as the National Organization for Women (NOW) and many black elected officials—Mondale was able to win the Democratic nomination.

Once he had secured the nomination, Mondale selected New York representative Geraldine Ferraro as his vice-presidential running mate in an effort to benefit from the "gender gap." According to feminists, women were becoming increasingly dissatisfied with Republican positions on domestic and foreign policy issues; thus an explicit appeal to women could provide the Democrats with the votes they needed to prevail in presidential elections. In point of fact, the theory of the gender gap included more than a little wishful thinking by Democrats and by feminists anxious to portray themselves as a powerful political force.

The actual political gender gap that had developed during the 1980 presidential election resulted less from women's attraction to the Democrats than from the fact that while both men and women left the Democratic party in large numbers, more male than female Democrats deserted.[18] In 1980 the Republicans received somewhat more support among women in general than did the Democrats: Reagan captured 47 percent of the women's vote to Carter's 45 percent, with the balance going to Anderson. But among white women, the Republicans far outpolled the

Democrats, with Reagan winning 52 percent to Carter's 39 percent. As strong as this performance was, however, the Republican margin over the Democrats among white males was spectacular: Reagan received 59 percent to Carter's 32 percent, a difference of 27 percentage points. The true source of the gender gap in 1980 thus was the large number of white men who abandoned the Democratic ticket. Nevertheless, orthodox Democratic doctrine prior to the 1984 election held that women's votes were the key to the party's resurgence in presidential elections.

In addition to naming the first woman to a major party's national ticket, Mondale made another dramatic move at the Democratic convention. In his acceptance speech, Mondale indicated that, if elected, he would raise taxes. This campaign promise presented obvious risks, but Mondale hoped it would help him hold together his coalition. What united liberals, labor, and blacks was their common dependence upon federal domestic spending programs. Reagan's tax and budget cuts had devastated these programs, and as long as the tax cuts remained in force, Congress could not undo the damage. By pledging to raise taxes, Mondale hoped to spur his constituents to greater efforts on his behalf.

Another unusual aspect of the 1984 presidential campaign was the prominent role played by Jesse Jackson. Jackson's 1984 candidacy was a challenge by clergy and protest leaders to the political hegemony of black elected officials as much as it was a bid for the presidency.[19] Mondale found it advisable to court Jackson's support publicly, and this cost him the votes of many conservative whites in the general election.

The result of the 1984 election was a landslide victory for

Ronald Reagan. Mondale's pledge to raise taxes alienated many middle-class voters; and once again, considerably more women gave their votes to Ronald Reagan than to the Democratic candidate.

1988: Racial Division

The eight candidates who entered the race for the 1988 Democratic nomination could be seen as representing the geological strata of the postwar Democratic party. Senator Paul Simon and Congressman Richard Gephardt expressed different aspects of the Democratic party's New Deal tradition. Gephardt appealed to the economic concerns of workers and farmers, while Simon proudly affirmed his attachment to public-sector solutions for the nation's problems. Senator Albert Gore of Tennessee spoke for the new South and the party's postwar commitment to a strong national defense. Then came Jesse Jackson, the heir of the civil rights struggle and other protest movements of the 1960s. He was followed by Senator Joseph Biden, Gary Hart, and Governor Bruce Babbitt, spokesmen for the Democratic neoliberalism of the 1970s and 1980s. They sought to win middle-class support by advocating efforts to promote American economic competitiveness and to streamline both defense and domestic programs.

The final candidate, Governor Michael Dukakis, sought to win support from all elements of the party while not offending independents and Republicans. To accomplish this, Dukakis stressed the themes of competence and leadership and sought to eschew commitments on substantive programs. In this way, he hoped to avoid the problems faced by Walter Mondale in 1984. Mondale had attempted to unite the Democrats by proposing programs that would serve the party's core constituencies, but he was overwhelmingly defeated in the general election by voters who resented the burdens these programs would impose upon them. Dukakis was able to pursue his strategy of vagueness because he could draw upon large campaign contributions from the Greek-American community and from firms that did business with the state government of Massachusetts.

In the months before the Democratic convention, all the contenders but Dukakis and Jackson were eliminated. The Hart and Biden candidacies were destroyed by media revelations. In the case of Hart, investigators from the *Miami Herald* uncovered evidence of an extramarital affair. Over the next several days, scores of reporters hounded Hart, bombarded him with questions about his personal life, and made it impossible for him to continue his campaign. Biden was forced to withdraw from the campaign after the release of a videotape (clandestinely prepared by the Dukakis campaign) demonstrated that Biden had plagiarized a speech from British Labour leader Neil Kinnock. Reporters then investigated Biden further and discovered that he had exaggerated his academic accomplishments and had also committed plagiarism while in law school. The candidacies of Simon, Gephardt, Gore, and Babbitt floundered when they were unable to attract support outside their own regional bases.

Dukakis entered the Democratic National Convention with the support of 70 percent of the delegates—well over the majority required for the nomination. Though Jackson had won only 30 percent of the delegates, he refused to acknowledge defeat. This put Dukakis in a difficult position.

Jackson demanded major concessions on the Democratic party platform, sought to play a major role in the campaign, and ultimately asserted a claim on the vice-presidential nomination. Jackson's implicit threat was to refuse to give the ticket his full support, which would cost the Democrats millions of black votes and lead to certain defeat in the general election. On the other hand, by making major concessions to Jackson, Dukakis could alienate millions of white voters.

In the end, Dukakis rejected Jackson's bid for the vice-presidential nomination, choosing instead Lloyd Bentsen, a conservative Texan, in an effort to boost the ticket in a state critical to Democratic prospects and to attract southern whites. Dukakis also refused to make more than minor concessions to Jackson on the platform. He did permit Jackson to play a major and visible role at the Democratic convention but kept him at a distance during the subsequent campaign. Jackson, unwilling to risk being blamed for a Democratic defeat, endorsed the ticket, though his support for it during the campaign was only lukewarm.

Despite Dukakis's efforts to avoid too close an association with Jackson, conservative whites—some believing that a deal had been struck giving Jackson a major role in a Dukakis administration—abandoned the Democrats and supported the Republican candidate, George Bush. Bush attacked Dukakis as a "Massachusetts liberal" who would raise taxes, weaken the nation's defense, and coddle criminals like furloughed murderer Willie Horton. For fear of alienating key Democratic constituencies, Dukakis could scarcely disavow his commitments to civil rights, civil liberties, and social programs. Thus despite Dukakis's efforts to avoid the problems faced by the Mondale campaign in

1984, he could not escape being depicted as a politician with commitments to constituencies and causes that could be served only at the expense of the taxpayer and middle America. Once again, the Democrats lost the presidential contest.

ELECTORAL STRATEGIES: THE RECONSTITUTED RIGHT

The second major coalition of forces to emerge from the wreckage of the New Deal order was the "reconstituted right." This coalition eventually came to consist of a politically reunified American business community; social and religious conservatives who were initially mobilized by George Wallace; and southern whites, northern blue-collar workers, and large segments of the suburban middle class. This coalition formed over a period of roughly twenty years and in two phases. The first phase, comprising the Nixon years, was the electoral era of the "silent majority." The second phase, coinciding with the ascendancy of Reagan, was the era of the fully reconstituted right.

1968 and 1972: The Silent Majority

In 1968 and 1972, Richard Nixon assembled a coalition of "the unyoung, the unpoor, and the unblack."[20] In other words, Nixon's coalition consisted of voters who were offended by or opposed to groups associated with the Democratic party. Two aspects of this effort are notable.

First, the coalition Nixon assembled was not—at least not

yet—united by philosophical or ideological principles beyond opposition to the Democrats. Nixon aides aptly termed it the "silent majority." It was, in fact, silent on matters of philosophy, led by a politician whose world view and vision were decidedly pragmatic. Many Nixon administration policies did not diverge from its Democratic predecessors'. In particular, social spending skyrocketed during Nixon's presidency and federal regulatory efforts greatly expanded. Nixon had constructed a successful electoral coalition without uniting voters around any affirmative ideology or program.

The second noteworthy aspect of the Nixon coalition was the role of business. The American business community united for Nixon against McGovern in 1972, but it had not been unanimous in its enthusiasm for Nixon in 1968 nor would it be in its support for Ford in 1976. The Nixon administration's trade policies alienated internationally competitive segments of the business community, such as multinational corporations and the banking industry. Business leaders in these sectors instead pursued a strategy of studied bipartisanship, symbolized by the formation of the Trilateral Commission, composed of prominent figures from America, Europe, and Japan.

By the 1976 presidential election, the coalition Nixon had assembled was fragmented. Many of its members, chastened by the Watergate revelations, returned to the Democratic party they had abandoned in 1972. Other members of Nixon's silent coalition continued to be an important element in American electoral politics. In 1980, this constituency was remobilized, reinforced, and finally given a voice by Ronald Reagan.

1980 and 1984: Reconstitution of the Right

In 1980, Reagan successfully sought to rebuild and expand the Nixon coalition. In contrast to Nixon, however, he presented a set of affirmative proposals designed to link his supporters to one another and to his presidential campaign. Reagan promised middle-class suburbanites that he would trim social programs, cut taxes, and bring inflation under control; he pledged to social and religious conservatives enactment of antiabortion and school prayer legislation; and he promised opponents of the civil rights revolution an end to federal support for affirmative action and minority quotas. Reagan also promised American business that he would relax the environmental rules and other regulations that Democrats had enacted during the 1970s, and he offered the defense industry greatly increased rates of military spending—this under the rubric of the need to respond to a growing Soviet threat.

Each of Reagan's themes—tax cuts, social service reductions, expanded military spending, relaxation of business regulations, and so on—was designed to link him to a major national political force. The main problem faced by the Reaganites was that these themes, whatever the case for them individually, were contradictory. The most important of these contradictions was between Reagan's promise of substantial tax relief for the middle class and his pledge to increase defense spending dramatically.

At this juncture, the Reaganites presented a political theory that, like the Democrats' industrial policy, masqueraded as economic doctrine. That theory was called "supply-side economics." The economic details of the theory need not concern us; indeed, most economists ridiculed it. However, like industrial policy, supply-side economics was far more important as a political than an economic doctrine. Supply-side theory purported to show that it was possible to cut taxes and increase spending simultaneously. When Reagan promised to introduce supply-side economics, he was asserting that he could and would pursue policies that worked to the advantage of divergent elements in his proposed constituency.

Once Reagan had resolved the contradictions in his political position by embracing supply-side economics, and promised to eviscerate Democratic regulatory programs, the stage was set for the political unification of American business under Republican auspices. The enthusiastic support of business provided the GOP with access to enormous campaign funds, sometimes laundered through conservative foundations and organizations. This gave the Republicans in 1980 a decisive edge in the use of expensive new political technologies—computers, phone banks, polls, and television advertising.

Under Reagan's leadership, the Republican party scored a decisive victory in the 1980 presidential election, won control of the Senate, and substantially increased its representation in the House. Once in office, Reagan sought to fashion a legislative program that would implement his campaign promises and solidify his relationship with the various groups that had helped bring him to power. In the first half of his term, he moved to cut taxes, reduce inflation, slash social programs, increase defense outlays, reduce federal regulatory controls over business, and diminish federal efforts on behalf of blacks and other minorities. In addition, Reagan gave his support—although more in word than deed—to social and religious conservatives who were determined to ban abortion and return prayer to the public schools.

Reagan's legislative efforts encountered a number of obstacles. First, efforts to reduce spending on domestic social problems were hampered by powerful political constituencies that effectively defended these programs. This was especially true in the case of Social Security, precisely the area where spending cuts might have yielded substantial budgetary savings. Second, Reagan's efforts to reduce regulatory controls over business, especially by placing limits on the federal agencies charged with environmental protection, encountered stiff resistance from environmentalists. They mobilized the iron triangle of congressional investigation, media disclosure, and judicial process that had become such a potent political weapon during the previous decade. This counterattack brought about the ouster of several Reagan appointees, most notably EPA administrator Ann Burford Gorsuch and Secretary of the Interior James Watt. The third problem the president faced was the budget deficit. The supply-side concept that Reagan had championed as a candidate may have been a brilliant political theory. But when he actually cut taxes and simultaneously increased defense outlays, while failing to realize commensurate savings in domestic social spending, the result was an enormous federal deficit, high real interest rates, and considerable unease in business and financial circles. These problems, in conjunction with the administration's stance on social issues, created tension between "movement conservatives" and more moderate elements of the Republican coalition.

Despite deficits and other problems, Reagan was able to fulfill many of his campaign promises during his first term

67

in office. The upper- and upper-middle classes realized substantial savings from Reagan's tax-reduction programs. Inflation was brought under control, although the cost of doing so was the deepest recession since the 1930s. Arms outlays increased dramatically. The federal regulatory climate became more favorable to business. The rate of increase in domestic social spending diminished, and the federal government's efforts on behalf of minorities and the poor were reduced. Finally, various federal agencies limited their backing for abortion, and Reagan personally continued to offer moral support and encouragement to social and religious conservatives.[21]

As a result of this record, Reagan's support among the forces that had initially elected him to office increased. In the 1984 election, Reagan's share of the vote rose within all the major segments of the electorate that had backed him in 1980. According to the *New York Times*/CBS News exit poll, Reagan's support between the 1980 and 1984 elections increased among southern whites by 11 points, to 72 percent; among Roman Catholics by 6 points, to 55 percent; among white born-again Christians by 17 points, to 80 percent; among middle- and upper-income voters by 7 points, to 65 percent; and among the elderly—many of whom live on fixed incomes and are extremely sensitive to inflation—by 9 points, to 63 percent. Despite the Democrats' nomination of Geraldine Ferraro, Reagan won 57 percent of the women's vote to Mondale's 42 percent; among white women, Reagan was supported by 64 percent to Mondale's 36 percent—a stunning 28-point Republican advantage. These increases enabled Reagan to win 59 percent of the popular vote in 1984 and to carry 49 states.[22]

1988: Confirming the Reagan Coalition

In 1988, six candidates competed for the Republican presidential nomination—Vice President George Bush, Senator Robert Dole, Governor Pierre DuPont, former secretary of state Alexander Haig, Representative Jack Kemp, and Reverend Pat Robertson. At the outset, the contest appeared to be wide open. Each candidate had ties to a major Republican constituency, and George Bush was widely considered to be a weak candidate. Indeed, commentators dismissed him as a "wimp." Bush, however, had ties to all the groups that Reagan had united, and this proved to be decisive. Bush easily secured the nomination, demonstrating the dominance of the Reagan coalition within the Republican party.

Bush was advised by his pollsters to select a young running mate who would attract the baby-boomers' vote, and he wanted a running mate who would strengthen his support on the Republican right wing; Bush chose Indiana Senator Dan Quayle. His decision immediately came under fire when the national media revealed that Quayle had avoided service in the Vietnam War by relying upon his family's influence to secure an appointment to the Indiana National Guard. Quayle's poor academic record also came under scrutiny, and he was widely characterized as an intellectual lightweight. His performance in the vice-presidential debate did nothing to dispel this image.

The apparent weakness of the Republican ticket convinced the Democrats that they had their best shot at victory in years. Dukakis had intended to prevent the race from focusing on ideology and planned instead to make the com-

69

petence of the candidates the major issue. The Bush campaign blocked this strategy by making heavy use of negative advertising to attack Dukakis's record as too liberal. At the same time, Bush followed the Reagan formula of bypassing journalists by eschewing news conferences and interviews and building his campaign around staged events. This infuriated journalists, who characterized the Bush campaign as devoid of issues and substance.

Bush's attack on Dukakis's liberalism helped him to maintain the unity of the Reagan coalition. Among southern whites, Bush won 64 percent of the vote to Dukakis's 32 percent. Among voters with a family income of $50,000 a year or more—who cast half the votes necessary for victory in 1988—Bush received 62 percent of the vote to Dukakis's 37 percent. White evangelicals gave Bush 81 percent of their vote and Dukakis only 18 percent. The only group that voted overwhelmingly for Dukakis were blacks, who awarded him 86 percent of their vote. As for the gender gap, Bush was somewhat less successful among female than male voters but nevertheless received 56 percent of the votes cast by white women compared to Dukakis's 43 percent.[23]

Overall, Bush won 54 percent of the popular vote and carried forty states. In the Electoral College, Bush's margin was 446 to 112. The magnitude of the Republican win in the Electoral College was, in part, a consequence of the dominance that the Republicans have enjoyed over the past twenty years in the South and in the Mountain states. It is likely that the Democrats will have difficulty surmounting this Electoral College advantage of the Republicans in the years to come. In the meantime, Democrats were left to ask themselves whether a party unable to defeat the ticket of Bush and Quayle could ever hope to capture the presidency.

THE CONGRESSIONAL ARENA

While the Republicans have dominated presidential elections for the past twenty years, the Democrats have maintained an equally strong grip on Congress. Four developments over the past two decades have enabled congressional Democrats to entrench themselves in office even as the Republicans were dominating the arena of presidential elections.

First, as discussed earlier, during the 1960s and 1970s Congress enacted many new programs for local economic development, housing, hospital construction, control of water pollution, education, social services, and other concerns. These programs make available tens of billions of dollars each year that members of Congress can channel into their constituencies. By using their influence over the allocation of these funds, incumbent representatives and senators can build political support for themselves at home. In this way, incumbents greatly enhance their prospects for reelection. Because the Democrats held a solid majority in Congress when this process began, it has helped to perpetuate their control.

Second, the flow of billions of federal dollars to state and local governments and nonprofit organizations has expanded the number and influence of individuals throughout the country associated with the public and not-for-profit sectors. These men and women have a large stake in the continuation of high levels of federal funding for do-

71

mestic programs and therefore in the election of congressional candidates with such a commitment. Republicans in Congress can usually be counted upon to pursue existing federal dollars for their districts, but Democratic representatives are considerably more likely to support new federal domestic initiatives as well as greater expenditures on current programs. Hence, Democratic congressional candidates throughout the nation—newcomers and incumbents alike—are usually able to recruit large numbers of energetic individuals from the public and nonprofit sectors to work in their campaigns. In presidential contests, which are fought mainly in the media, campaign workers are not of decisive importance. In lower-visibility congressional, state, and local elections, however, they can be; therefore, the greater depth of the Democratic party is of particular importance here.[24] The media are more important in Senate than House races, which helps explain why the Republicans are at less of a disadvantage in elections to the upper chamber.

Third, the Democrats' ability to maintain their congressional majorities is enhanced by the strength of the party's base in state and local government. As noted previously, Democratic control of state legislatures has led congressional district lines to be drawn in ways that favor the Democrats. In addition, because the Democrats are able to draw on a larger pool of public officials than the Republicans, they are often able to field candidates with greater visibility and political experience in senatorial races and contests for open House seats.

Finally, because members of Congress devote so much effort to maximizing the flow of federal funds to their constituencies, voters have come to judge congressional candidates largely in terms of their ability to deliver these benefits. While voters expect presidential candidates to articulate national interests, they want their representatives in Congress to protect their particular interests.[25] Congressional Democrats have, on the whole, been more effective in this respect than their Republican colleagues. Voters have therefore elected Republican presidential candidates who promised to slash domestic spending and also regularly returned Democratic representatives who could be counted on to fight for more federal dollars for their favorite programs.

For a brief period during the late 1970s and early 1980s, it appeared that the Republicans were developing a means of challenging the Democratic lock on Congress. The Republicans constructed a national fund-raising apparatus of unprecedented size and efficiency. During the 1980 elections, the Republican party raised and spent approximately $85 million on behalf of its congressional and senatorial candidates. Democratic party committees, by contrast, were able to raise only some $17 million. In addition to providing money to GOP House and Senate candidates, the Republican national apparatus also supplied them with technical assistance—polling, phone banks, direct-mail specialists, and media consultants. Moreover, the centralized campaign apparatus the Republicans built enabled the party to deploy its resources where they could be most effective, against weak incumbent Democrats and in contests involving open seats. In 1980, these innovations helped the Republicans win control in the Senate and greatly increase their representation in the House.[26]

By 1984, however, the Democrats were able to effectively counter the Republican challenge. Under the leadership of Representative Tony Coelho, the Democrats launched a concerted drive to raise money from business PACs. Coelho reminded business leaders that it was all but certain that the Democrats would retain control over the House and that consequently corporate executives would find themselves dealing with Democratic committee and subcommittee chairmen after the election. Thus it would be

FIGURE 2.3
PAC CONTRIBUTIONS TO CONGRESSIONAL
CANDIDATES, 1978–1988

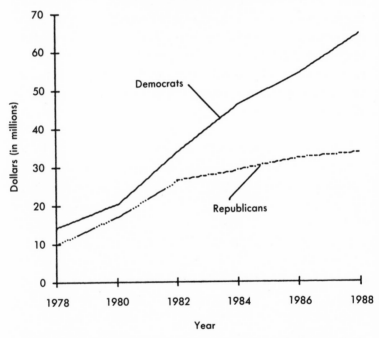

SOURCE: 1978–1986, *Statistical Abstract of the United States* (Washington, D.C.: U.S. Government Printing Office, 1988), 254; 1988, *Congressional Quarterly Weekly Report,* vol. 47, no. 9 (4 March 1989): 478.

risky for them to be guided solely by their personal partisan and ideological preferences when making political contributions.[27] In this way, as figure 2.3 indicates, the Democrats increased their share of campaign contributions from PACs and countered the Republican party's centralized fund-raising apparatus. This helped the Democrats to minimize the impact on Congress of the Republican presidential landslide of 1984, to recapture the Senate in 1986, and even to increase their strength in both chambers in the face of George Bush's 1988 presidential victory.

For these reasons, the Democrats have been able to maintain their control of Congress despite the reconstitution of the political right and Republican hegemony in the presidential arena during the 1980s. Both parties also have extended their power into other institutions of American government—the Democratics by using their base in Congress and the GOP by taking advantage of its stronghold in the White House.

3

The Democrats and the Domestic State

THE DEMOCRATS AND REPUBLICANS HAVE in recent decades established links with different segments of the nation's governmental apparatus. The Democrats have entrenched themselves in Congress, federal social service, labor and regulatory agencies, and government bureaucracies and nonprofit organizations on the state and local levels that help administer national social programs. The Democrats' base has its roots in the events of the 1930s and 1960s, and, reinforced by the party's hold on Congress, has become so well established that it can withstand Republican control of the White House. Together, these developments have transformed the Democrats from a political force based on local party machines into one grounded in Congress and the domestic state.

The Republicans, as we shall see in subsequent chapters, have sought to entrench themselves in the White House, the national security apparatus, sectors of the economy that benefit from military spending, and those segments of American society whose income, autonomy, or values are threatened by the welfare and regulatory state built by the

Democrats. This competitive entrenchment by the Republicans and Democrats has to a considerable extent replaced mass electoral mobilization as a means of securing power in the United States today and helps explain how high levels of partisan conflict can coexist with low rates of voting participation in contemporary American politics.

FORMS OF DEMOCRATIC ENTRENCHMENT

Since the 1930s, Democratic presidents and Congresses have secured the enactment of a large number of social and regulatory programs. To administer these programs, they created or expanded such agencies as Health and Human Services (HHS), the Department of Labor (DOL), and the Environmental Protection Agency (EPA). These bureaucracies are linked by grants-in-aid to public agencies and nonprofit organizations at the state and local levels and through these to the Democratic party's mass base.[1] This entire complex is tied to Democrats in Congress, who affirm the worth of federal social and regulatory programs and defend the authority and budgets of the agencies responsible for their administration.

There are three ways in which federal social and regulatory agencies serve as centers of influence for the Democrats even when the White House is controlled by the Republicans. First, individuals who work in agencies such as HHS—and their counterparts in the state, local and nonprofit sectors—are likely to have Democratic loyalties.[2] When agencies that provide such benefits as health care and welfare hire employees, they quite properly seek and attract individuals who by personal belief and training are committed to these organizations' goals, and a commitment to the public sector is more likely to be found among Democrats than Republicans. The Democrats' defense of social programs and expenditures has over time reproduced and reinforced the attachment of public employees to that party. In turn, the millions of Americans who work in domestic public-sector occupations are an important source of votes and campaign support for the Democrats. The majority of them—over 60 percent in 1984—vote Democratic.[3] In addition, individuals who are active in Democratic campaigns are drawn heavily from state and local governments, universities, and other nonprofit institutions.

Second, federal domestic programs and agencies enable the Democrats to establish links with groups and forces throughout the nation. These bureaucratic networks have largely supplanted party organizations as the instruments through which Democrats in Washington are tied to a popular base. Since the New Deal era, the Democratic party has channeled benefits to a plethora of interests.[4] The beneficiaries of this largesse, of course, have reason to reward the Democrats with their political support. For the past half century, Democrats have thus been able to win strong backing from unionized workers and ethnic minorities—and even some middle-class homeowners, professionals, and members of the business community. Generally speaking, the more dependent members of a group are on federal domestic spending programs, the more likely they are to vote Democratic. In the 1988 presidential election, for example, 62 percent of voters with annual family incomes under $12,500 supported Dukakis, whereas only 37 percent of voters with incomes above $50,000 did so.[5]

Finally, the Democratic party's entrenchment in domestic agencies provides Democrats in Congress with administrative capabilities that endure even when they lose control of the presidency. The career employees of federal social and regulatory agencies have an enduring commitment to public-sector programs championed by the Democrats; these employees work with Democrats in Congress to maintain and protect such programs. The support of these agency employees enables the Democrats to retain substantial influence over the implementation of major areas of public policy, and to play a significant role in the nation's governance, even when a Republican occupies the White House.

With the support of congressional Democrats, agencies that administer federal social and regulatory programs often resist efforts by Republican presidents to redirect or limit their activities. For example, when the Reagan administration attempted to reorient EPA policies, it encountered stiff opposition from members of the agency's staff. Agency employees leaked information to Congress and the media—leaks that led to a series of congressional investigations and ultimately resulted in the ouster of Ann Burford Gorsuch, Reagan's EPA chief. As a result of this controversy, Reagan was compelled to appoint a new administrator, William Ruckleshaus, who was seen as likely to return the agency to its former course.

ORIGINS OF DEMOCRATIC ENTRENCHMENT: THE NEW DEAL

Democrats' links to federal social welfare and regulatory agencies date from the 1930s, when President Franklin

Roosevelt sought to institutionalize the New Deal. By establishing a base in agencies of the national government, New Deal liberals undertook not only to counter the influence of the conservative machine politicians and southern oligarchs who formerly dominated the party but also to strengthen the Democrats in their competition with the Republicans. New Deal liberals thus began the process through which the Democrats became a party grounded in governmental bureaucracies rather than local organizations.

The multitude of new agencies—the famous "alphabet agencies"—created to administer New Deal programs initially were viewed as temporary and were located outside the regular governmental structure. But in the mid-1930s, Roosevelt moved to make them permanent features of the American governmental system. Chronologically and politically, Roosevelt's effort belonged to the second phase of the New Deal—the phase extending from the Wagner Act and Social Security Act of 1935, through the Reorganization Act of 1937, to the congressional purge of 1938. The Reorganization Act was an effort to institutionalize the programs of FDR's first term by creating two new cabinet departments (to administer the public welfare and public works programs that had been enacted between 1933 and 1936) and by granting the president the authority to integrate other New Deal programs into the existing departmental structure.[6]

The reforms of 1935–1938 also helped to institutionalize the power of the Democrats by establishing direct links between the administration and a mass constituency. These links were accomplished by the National Labor Relations Act, which established procedures for organizing workers into unions, and the Social Security Act, which established a bureaucracy to provide benefits to Americans in times of need. Such assistance had formerly been provided, if at all, only by political machines.

Significantly, under amendments to the Social Security Act adopted in 1939, the Social Security Board required states to establish merit systems for the employees who administered the program on the state and local level; this requirement led to the creation of the first civil service systems in most states of the union.[7] The New Dealers sought through this requirement to ensure that control of the program would not be seized by whatever political forces happened to be dominant locally. New Dealers wanted the flow of these new benefits to be controlled from the center so that the political advantages of the program would accrue to the national Democratic administration that enacted it.

Roosevelt also undertook through his 1937 executive reorganization bill to extend White House control over the entire federal administrative apparatus, but he was not entirely successful. FDR's reorganization plan sought to expand the White House staff, create a central planning agency in the executive office, and place all administrative agencies, including the independent regulatory commissions, under one of the cabinet departments.

Opponents of the New Deal resisted Roosevelt's efforts to centralize in the White House control over the executive branch. FDR was forced to accept a compromise: Executive agencies retained a measure of independence, and Congress continued to exercise significant influence over the bureaucracy. Executive agencies were therefore left free to cultivate their own political alliances with interest groups and members of Congress. Ironically, it was the defeat of Roosevelt's efforts to strengthen White House control over the bureaucracy that made it possible for congressional Democrats in the 1970s and 1980s to retain substantial influence over administrative agencies in the face of Republican dominance of the presidency.

Administrative Entrenchment and Party Decline

Roosevelt's moves toward centralization began the transformation of the Democrats from a party dependent on an extensive network of political clubs and organizations to one grounded in administrative institutions. After the 1930s, the Democrats relied increasingly on administrative rather than party channels to establish links with their constituencies, to recruit and retain the loyalty of party activists, and to implement their party's programs. Eventually, the Democrats became so firmly entrenched in segments of the national administrative apparatus and its state and local counterparts that even loss of control of the White House was not sufficient to dislodge them.

Roosevelt was determined to entrench his followers in the national governmental apparatus because, in many states and localities, the Democratic party machinery was in the hands of his factional rivals and in others it was too weak to be politically useful to him. By strengthening bureaucratic institutions, and tying them closely to his cause, FDR sought to create a national apparatus through which he could mobilize political support and govern.[8]

On the state and local levels, FDR's endeavor to centralize and control the national government was supported by

83

middle-class liberals, who had a particular interest in substituting bureaucratic for partisan modes of organization. New Deal liberals wanted the government to play an active role in society, and bureaucracies are better suited than patronage machines to perform tasks requiring technical proficiency. By replacing patronage practices with personnel systems based on competitive examinations, bureaucratization would also skew the distribution of public jobs to the advantage of the public-sector professionals—teachers, social workers, and so on—who were an important element of the liberal constituency.[9]

Roosevelt's efforts generated major struggles, on state and local levels, between political forces committed to the national administration and incumbent Democratic leaders. Conflicts occurred in some states while FDR was still in the White House; in other states they did not erupt until fifteen or twenty years after his death.[10] The timing and character of these struggles for power depended upon the stance that local party leaders took toward the national administration and the techniques the leaders employed to maintain their power.

Where incumbent machine politicians supported the New Deal (as in Chicago and Pittsburgh), FDR was perfectly willing to distribute the patronage generated by New Deal programs through local party machines.[11] Where the incumbent Democratic leadership was hostile to the national administration and commanded a broadly based, patronage-oriented party machine (such as Tammany Hall in New York City), the president's followers organized through third-party movements or reform clubs (such as the American Labor party and later the Democratic reform movement in New York).[12] Finally, where the local Democratic leadership was hostile or indifferent to the New Deal and did not command a mass-based party organization (as in Michigan and Minnesota), Roosevelt loyalists were able with little difficulty to take over the Democratic caucus structure by allying with labor unions and farm organizations that had benefited from New Deal programs.[13] In these states, factional struggles within the Democratic party took the form of a straight ideological conflict between New Deal liberals and conservative Democrats.

By the 1960s, these struggles had given the Democrats an institutionally heterogeneous structure. Traditional patronage-oriented party organizations remained important in many states and localities, particularly in the Northeast and lower Midwest.[14] Labor unions continued to play an important role in party affairs.[15] At the same time, a number of federal, state, and local bureaucracies had come to be major Democratic party bastions.

THE 1960S AND 1970S

During the 1960s and 1970s, traditional party organizations were almost completely obliterated, labor unions were weakened, and the Democratic party became more fully dependent on its base of power in the domestic state. The efforts of a coalition of middle-class liberals and blacks to enhance their influence in American government and politics were largely responsible for this shift. To this end they abandoned accommodations in which they had formerly participated and allies with whom they formerly had been associated in the realms of civil rights and social policy, national security policy, and regulatory policy. In addition, they sought to rewrite the rules of the Democratic party and to alter the administrative procedures of the federal government so as to increase their own influence.

Civil Rights and Social Policy

One of the major accommodations underlying the New Deal coalition involved civil rights. Southern votes were crucial to the Democratic party's fortunes in the 1930s and 1940s, and therefore Roosevelt had avoided challenging the southern caste system. The emergence of a vigorous black civil rights movement in the 1950s and 1960s, however, made it impossible to ignore the issue of race any longer. Northern Democratic liberals were sympathetic to the plight of blacks and, at the same time, found in the issue of civil rights a means of discrediting their opponents within the Democratic party—initially southern conservatives, and subsequently working-class ethnics in the North. A similar mix of considerations underlay the urban programs of the New Frontier and Great Society.

As a number of scholars have noted, the major urban programs of the New Frontier and Great Society were drafted not in response to demands from their presumed beneficiaries—black slum dwellers—but rather on the initiative of presidentially appointed task forces.[16] The members of these task forces were mainly "professional reformers"—academics, foundation officials, senior civil servants, representatives of professional associations, and so forth.[17] Presidents Kennedy and Johnson were receptive to proposals of this sort if for no other reason than to retain the support of this important element of the party's national constituency.

Middle-class liberals were considerably less influential on the local level. In many large cities after World War II, a rather stable accommodation had been achieved among party politicians, businessmen, union leaders, newspaper publishers, middle-income homeowners, and the ethnic working classes. Writing in the early 1960s, Robert Salisbury described this pattern as "the new convergence of power," and roughly speaking, these forces converged around a program of urban renewal in the central business district for the business community and construction unions, low taxes for homeowners, and secure jobs in the municipal civil service for the lower-middle class and upwardly mobile members of the working class.[18] Upper-middle-class professionals had some influence over municipal agencies, although their influence was constrained by the desire of mayors to keep taxes low and of municipal employees to control their own work routines and determine the standards that would govern the hiring, promotion, and firing of civil servants.

Upper-middle-class liberals wanted to increase their influence over municipal agencies; to this end, they sought to use the access they enjoyed to the Kennedy and Johnson administrations to circumvent the local convergence of power. The presidential task forces that drafted New Frontier and Great Society legislation argued that municipal

87

bureaucracies did not command the resources, the talent, or the initiative that was necessary to solve the "urban crisis." To deal with this problem they proposed to extend federal grants-in-aid to local governments to support "innovative" programs.

To obtain these federal grants, cities found it necessary to establish independent agencies that would be controlled by local counterparts of the Washington officials who dispensed this money, to have existing municipal departments contract with consulting firms, or to hire administrators who shared the outlook or knew the vocabulary of the dispensers of federal grants. The "grantsmen" who were most successful in obtaining federal funds naturally were those whose educational backgrounds, social origins, and institutional affiliations were similar to the federal grant givers, and who proposed to spend federal monies for purposes their Washington counterparts favored. In other words, the federal grant-in-aid programs initiated by the Kennedy and Johnson administrations allowed upper-middle-class professionals and their political allies, by using their access to the White House, to extend their influence over the policies, programs, and hiring practices of municipal agencies. As figure 3.1 indicates, federal grants-in-aid to state and local governments expanded dramatically during the 1960s and 1970s.

Blacks were important allies in the liberals' battle for control of these agencies. Liberals denounced municipal bureaucracies as "insensitive" and "unresponsive" to the needs of the black community. Blacks had strong reasons to join this attack: The mechanisms of community participation that were attached to Great Society programs provided them with channels through which they could both influ-

FIGURE 3.1
FEDERAL GRANTS-IN-AID TO STATE AND LOCAL
GOVERNMENTS, 1960–1988*

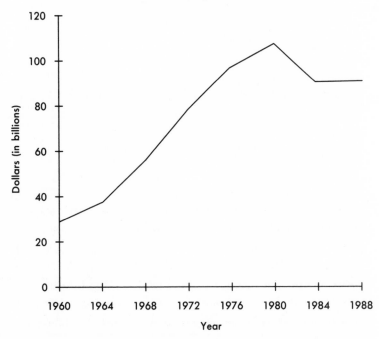

SOURCE: Office of Management and Budget, *Budget of the United States Government, Fiscal Year 1990, Historical Tables* (Washington, D.C.: U.S. Government Printing Office, 1989), table 12–2.
*Grants are in constant 1982 dollars.

ence the way municipal departments distributed their benefits and obtain access to the patronage controlled by federally-funded community action agencies, model cities boards, neighborhood service centers, and community development corporations. These mechanisms of community participation, furthermore, legitimized federal intervention in local affairs and provided an institutional framework through which blacks could be organized to provide local political support for these programs.[19]

National Security Policy

Factional struggles within the Democratic party intensified after Lyndon B. Johnson escalated the war in Vietnam. Vietnam turned upper-middle-class liberal Democrats against the White House and transformed the struggle for influence at the periphery of the political system into an all-out battle for control at the center. In the late 1960s, liberals launched a full-scale attack on the national security establishment. They strongly disapproved of how American military power was being used and argued that the funds spent on weapons could better be used to meet pressing domestic needs. Of course, such a reordering of national priorities would also direct the flow of federal funds toward government agencies over which liberals exercised influence—and away from the political forces the liberals now opposed.

Opponents of American military and national security policy began to sharply criticize practices that previously had aroused little journalistic attention or public opposition: the Pentagon's tolerance of cost overruns in weapons procurement contracts, the public relations campaigns and lobbying efforts of the Pentagon, the hiring of retired military officers by defense contractors, the failure of Congress to monitor the activities of the CIA and other intelligence agencies. Liberals sought to subject the "military-industrial complex" to stricter external control and to limit the role it had come to play in the nation's life during the Cold War years.

By attacking these practices, liberals were attempting to disrupt the set of compromises that Presidents Roosevelt and Harry Truman had arranged during World War II and the Cold War—a foreign policy consensus in which liberals at the time had been enthusiastic participants. The construction of a permanent military apparatus in the 1940s and 1950s made it possible to give all the major actors in American politics a stake in national security policies. Members of Congress were given access to a huge pork barrel, which incumbents could use to enhance their political security.[20] National defense made it politically possible for public expenditures to be maintained at a level that kept unemployment reasonably low, wages reasonably high, and labor reasonably happy. And through the procurement of weapons and supplies, those elements of the American business community that had been most strongly identified with the isolationist wing of the Republican party were reconciled to internationalism and big government.

The post-Vietnam attack on the national security sector was quite successful, and defense spending as a percentage of GNP dropped sharply through the 1970s (see figure 3.2). Especially after the 1979 Soviet invasion of Afghanistan, however, conservative Republicans were able to charge that their opponents had dangerously weakened the nation's defenses and in this way to rally support for a major military buildup. The Republicans were able to cultivate support in regions of the country—the South and West—and among interests in the business community with a stake in defense spending.

FIGURE 3.2
U.S. DEFENSE SPENDING AS A PERCENTAGE OF
GNP, 1960–1980

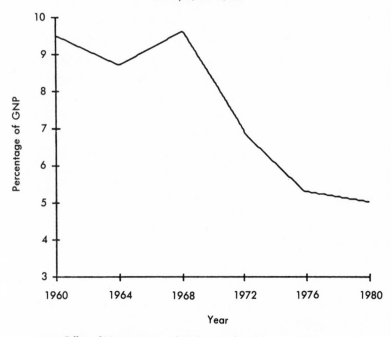

SOURCE: Office of Management and Budget, *Budget of the United States, Fiscal Year 1990, Historical Tables* (Washington, D.C.: U.S. Government Printing Office, 1989), table 3–2.

The New Regulation

The 1960s and 1970s witnessed a major expansion of the regulatory activities of the federal government. Liberal consumer advocates, environmentalists, and their supporters in Congress asserted that existing regulatory agencies had been captured by business; they proposed major reforms that promised both to better protect the public and to enhance their own political influence.[21]

These consumer advocates and environmentalists undertook to alter the procedures and practices of regulatory agencies so that the agencies would serve broader public interests rather than the interests of business. In particular, these activists sought to limit the interchange of personnel between agencies and the interests they regulated; the cocoon of minimum rates, entry restrictions, public subsidies, and tax benefits that had been placed around the transportation and energy sectors of the economy; and the mutually beneficial relationships that had developed among executive agencies, congressional committees, and private interests. Such groups as Common Cause, Ralph Nader's Public Citizen, and the Natural Resources Defense Council attempted to end these practices and increase their own influence in the regulatory process by sponsoring sunshine laws, by subjecting regulatory agencies to close judicial supervision, and by providing for the representation of public-interest groups in the administrative process.

In addition, consumer and environmental activists insisted that the federal government undertake major new programs to deal with such problems as air and water pollution, product safety, and health hazards associated with food and drugs. Between 1966 and 1976, these activists were able to secure the enactment of dozens of new regulatory statutes, greatly expanding the federal government's role in the economy. In contrast to the typical New Deal regulatory program which encompassed a single industrial sector, such as trucking or airlines, the "new regulation" of the 1960s and 1970s affected firms throughout the economy. To administer these programs, Congress created a number of new federal regulatory agencies such as the EPA, the Consumer Product Safety Commission, and the Occupational Health and Safety Administration.[22] These agencies and the congressional committees that oversee and protect them subsequently became major Democratic bastions with substantial influence over the domestic economy.

Party and Administrative Reform

During the 1960s, liberal political forces also significantly changed the structure and practices of the Democratic party.[23] The party reforms enacted after the antiwar candidates were defeated at the 1968 Democratic National Convention were the most comprehensive since the Progressive Era. Chief among them were rules requiring that delegations to future national conventions be composed of blacks, women, and youths in a "reasonable relationship to their presence in the population of the state." Other important reforms encouraged states to select convention delegations through primary elections or open caucus procedures and discouraged the slatemaking efforts of party organizations. Groups such as Common Cause also sponsored reforms in the area of campaign finance, including public subsidies to presidential candidates, limitations on individual contributions, and public disclosure of the names of contributors.

Through these reforms, liberals weakened the position of their major competitors within the Democratic camp—urban politicians, labor and business leaders—and enhanced the importance of middle-class issue-oriented activists and racial minorities.[24] Moreover, the political reforms of the 1960s and 1970s all but destroyed what remained of local party organizations. This left the Democrats more fully dependent upon their bastions within the domestic state.

In addition to party reform, liberal Democrats sought to secure a number of major reforms in governmental and bureaucratic organization. They modified the public personnel system, which had been built around competitive examinations and a career civil service, by advocating various mechanisms of affirmative action, and by delegating many public tasks to nongovernmental institutions whose employees were not career civil servants. Prior to these reforms, the New Dealers had drawn support from a middle class and an upwardly mobile working class whose members could expect to secure civil service jobs through competitive examinations; Democratic liberals in the 1960s and 1970s sought to win the support of blacks who had been excluded from public jobs by such examinations, and of an upper-middle class that had little interest in moving slowly up the ladder in career civil service systems. The former would benefit from affirmative action programs, and the latter stood to gain if public responsibilities were delegated and public monies were allocated to the institutions with which they were affiliated—nonprofit social service agencies, legal service clinics, public interest law firms, and so forth.

After their break with the Johnson administration, and after the defeats in the 1968 and 1972 presidential elections, liberal Democrats lost the access to the presidency they previously had enjoyed. Consequently, they opposed reforms that would increase presidential control over the executive branch, such as those proposed by the Ash Coun-

cil in 1970, or the ones President Nixon sought to implement by fiat in 1973. They hoped instead to reduce the
powers of the presidency and to increase the influence
within the administrative process of the institutions with
which they were allied or to which they enjoyed access.

Liberal political forces also used their access to national
news media to influence the behavior of executive agencies
through investigative reporting and Naderite exposés.
Similarly, environmental, consumer, and civil rights groups
attempted to subject administrative agencies to tighter
court supervision; these groups commanded considerable
legal talent, and the federal judiciary in the 1960s and
1970s loosened requirements for standing, narrowed the
scope of the doctrine of political questions, and enriched
the range of remedies it was prepared to consider in class
action suits.[25] Finally, after decades of seeking to limit the
powers of Congress, Democrats in the 1970s sought to
expand Congress's power over the administration—especially in the areas of budgeting, investigations, and executive privilege—because of the access they enjoyed to that
body.

For the very reason that these efforts to reorder national
priorities and alter government processes were part and
parcel of a struggle for political power in the United
States, they sparked major conflicts. It may seem paradoxi-
cal, then, that the political turbulence of the 1960s and
1970s was accompanied by a marked decline in voter
turnout rates. The explanation for this apparent paradox is
that the liberal Democrats' strategies of bureaucratic warfare during this period served as a substitute for party
building. Rather than build mass organizations and mobilize voters, Democrats sought to entrench themselves in

major segments of the domestic state. This provided an opening that Richard Nixon, Ronald Reagan, and George Bush would later exploit.

BUREAUCRATIC ENTRENCHMENT VERSUS VOTER MOBILIZATION

During the 1960s and 1970s, a coalition of liberals and blacks within the Democratic party took the initiative in expanding federal social and regulatory programs and reforming governmental procedures. These efforts were in part related to factional conflicts among Democrats and were at times resisted by other elements of the party, such as southern conservatives, organized labor, and old-line urban politicians.

During the Reagan-Bush era, however, such factional divisions have been less evident. In response to the threat that a resurgent GOP presents to them all, the major components of the Democratic party have striven to overcome their differences and to unite in defense of those domestic programs and agencies they all can support. In recent budget battles, congressional Democrats have displayed unusual unity in opposing White House efforts to cut domestic expenditures and maintain spending on the military. Indeed, in recent years Democrats in the House and Senate have taken the extraordinary step of delegating to the congressional party leadership the authority to negotiate a budget agreement with the White House and then have lined up solidly behind the resulting revenue and expenditure decisions.[26] This dramatic reversal of the trend of increasing decentralization in Congress is also reflected in roll-call votes. Over the course of the 1980s, as figure 3.3 indicates, Democrats displayed increasing cohesion in roll-call voting in the House of Representatives. Party voting in the Senate followed a similar path.

Congressional Democrats have united in defense of do-

FIGURE 3.3
DEMOCRATIC UNITY IN THE HOUSE OF
REPRESENTATIVES, 1968–1988*

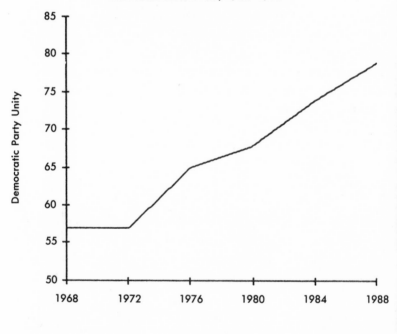

Year

SOURCE: *Congressional Quarterly Weekly Report,* vol. 46, no. 47 (19 Nov. 1988): 3338.
*Party unity is defined as the percentage of Democrats who vote with their party on issues that divide the two parties.

98

mestic programs and agencies because these have become central bastions of the party. Persons affiliated with federal domestic agencies, and with the state and municipal bureaucracies and nonprofit organizations linked to them, vote disproportionately for the Democrats and provide the party with a major portion of its activists. In addition, federal

FIGURE 3.4
FEDERAL SOCIAL SPENDING AND DEMOCRATIC
VOTE MOBILIZATION, 1960–1988*

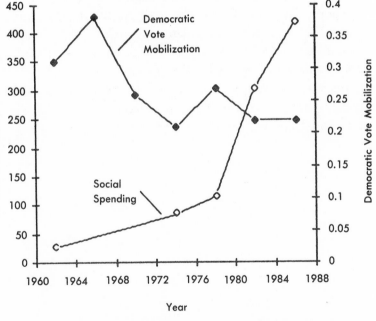

SOURCE: Office of Management and Budget, *Budget of the United States Government, Fiscal Year 1990, Historical Tables,* table 3–1; *Statistical Abstract of the United States* (Washington, D.C.: U.S. Government Printing Office, 1989), 240, 259.
*Democratic vote mobilization is the total vote for the Democratic presidential candidate as a proportion of the voting-age population. Federal social expenditures exclude Social Security and are in constant 1982 dollars.

social and regulatory agencies are notable centers of resistance to Republican efforts to shape national policy. Finally, domestic programs and agencies, in conjunction with the party's control of Congress, provide the Democrats with a continuing governing capacity despite their diminishing ability to mobilize votes in the arena of presidential elections.

As figure 3.4 indicates, federal spending (adjusted for inflation) on social programs defended by the Democrats has continued to rise over the past quarter century despite declining Democratic vote mobilization in presidential elections. Thus, the Democrats have become increasingly entrenched in social and regulatory agencies of the domestic state at the same time that the party's capacity to mobilize large numbers of voters has declined.

Because federal domestic programs and agencies have become such important Democratic bastions, the Republicans laid siege to them during the 1980s.

4

The Republican Offensive

SINCE WINNING CONTROL of the presidency in 1980, the Republicans have worked to undermine Democratic strongholds and to create a constellation of institutions, policies, and political forces to solidify their power. The principal weapons the GOP has deployed against its opponents are domestic spending cuts, tax reductions, and deregulation. These weapons have weakened important institutional bastions of the Democratic party and disrupted the social groups and forces upon which it depends for support. At the same time, through national security, monetary, and fiscal policy, the Republicans have undertaken to reorganize social forces and establish mechanisms of governance to maintain their rule.

These disparate strategies are not components of some master plan that the Republicans devised prior to gaining power. Rather, they emerged in the course of conflicts both within the GOP and between the White House and institutions controlled by the Democrats. The Republicans' political weapons have been shaped not only by the victories they have achieved but also by the compromises the GOP has

101

been compelled to make and the defeats it has suffered in these struggles.

DISRUPTING DEMOCRATIC INSTITUTIONS

The Republicans have worked to weaken social service and regulatory agencies in which the Democrats are entrenched. The Reagan and Bush administrations have promoted tax reductions, domestic spending cuts, and efforts at deregulation to limit these agencies' powers. These Republican policies have reduced the extractive, distributive, and regulatory capabilities of institutions over which the Democrats exercise influence. This has diminished the Democrats' ability to achieve their policy objectives, overcome divisions in their coalition, and provide benefits to groups allied with the party.

In 1981 the Reagan administration sponsored legislation that substantially cut individual and corporate income tax rates and indexed these rates to inflation. Congressional Democrats responded to the administration's bill by introducing a proposal of their own. A bidding war ensued, and the tax bill that was enacted reduced revenues more sharply than the White House had planned. Coupled with the administration's military buildup and inability to secure reductions in domestic spending as drastic as it had proposed, these tax cuts produced the enormous budget deficits of the 1980s. As figure 4.1 illustrates, the federal government's annual deficit increased from approximately $60 billion at the end of the Carter administration to a peak of over $200 billion during the Reagan presidency. Annual deficits

FIGURE 4.1
THE FEDERAL BUDGET DEFICIT, 1978–1988

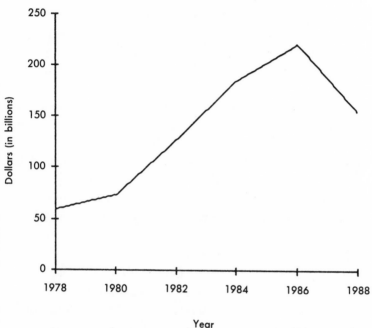

SOURCE: Office of Management and Budget, *Budget of the United States Government, Fiscal Year 1990, Historical Tables* (Washington, D.C.: U.S. Government Printing Office, 1989), table 15–6.

began to decline from that peak in the late 1980s, although the decline was largely a result of surpluses in the Social Security trust fund.

Five years later, in the 1986 tax reform act, tax rates were further reduced and numerous loopholes—deductions, exemptions, and tax preferences—were eliminated from the federal tax code. By closing the loopholes for influential groups that had made nominally high income tax rates politically feasible, the 1986 tax reform act has made it difficult for Congress to restore any of the lost revenues. Thus when seeking to reduce the budget deficit at the beginning of the Bush administration, Congress was only able to consider increasing those taxes that produce little in the way of revenue, such as those on alcohol, gasoline, and tobacco.

These restrictions on the extractive capacities of Congress have impaired that institution's distributive capabilities. Because the federal government has been strapped for revenues, funding levels for existing programs have come under pressure and it has been all but impossible for congressional Democrats to enact new social programs, despite demands that more be done to cope with such problems as the AIDS epidemic and homelessness.[1]

Republican tax policies have also exacerbated cleavages within the Democratic party. During the New Deal and postwar decades, many groups made claims on the federal treasury; their claims were accommodated through logrolling arrangements that characteristically were negotiated by the Democratic leadership of Congress. These arrangements entailed a steady growth of the public sector through a process of budgetary "incrementalism," as Aaron Wildavsky then called it.[2] This pattern of policy making depended on a steady expansion of public revenues, which was achieved—without the political conflict that would have resulted from repeated increases in nominal tax rates—by allowing inflation to steadily increase real rates of federal income taxation through what came to be called "bracket creep."

By slashing federal tax rates and introducing indexation

104

to prevent bracket creep, the Republicans have undermined the fiscal foundations of the New Deal pattern of accommodations among the beneficiaries of federal expenditure programs. The enormous deficit created by Republican fiscal policies exerts constant pressure on the funding levels of domestic programs. To protect their favorite programs in this fiscal environment, lobbyists representing such groups as farmers, organized labor, senior citizens, advocates of welfare spending, and local government officials have been compelled to engage in zero-sum conflict, in contrast to the positive-sum politics of the New Deal and postwar systems. One group's gain now has become another group's loss.[3] This state of affairs has placed strains on the Democratic coalition.

The 1989 outcry over catastrophic health insurance for the elderly illustrates how Reaganite fiscal policies have altered the political environment in which Congress operates. To avoid an increase in either tax rates or the deficit, Congress found it necessary to impose the costs of the new coverage on the program's beneficiaries. This generated a firestorm of protest among the elderly, compelling Congress to curtail the program. Thus members of Congress discovered that under the new Republican fiscal regime the enactment of new spending measures is no longer a sure means of winning political support.

Widespread concern about drug abuse has provided the Republicans with another avenue for undermining Democratic programs and agencies. As conceived by the Bush administration, the war on drugs would divert billions of dollars from social services to law-enforcement agencies. If Republicans succeed in redefining the central problem of

105

inner-city neighborhoods as drug abuse and the breakdown of law and order—rather than discrimination and unemployment—they could succeed in institutionalizing this shift in budgetary priorities.

After gaining control of the White House in the 1980s, the Republicans also undertook to restrict the regulatory capabilities of the federal government. They promoted deregulation in the transportation, energy, banking, and financial sectors of the economy, and they curtailed enforcement of environmental, health, safety, consumer, and antitrust laws. Regulatory agencies are consequently less likely to intervene against business on behalf of groups disadvantaged by market processes. For example, financial deregulation and the relaxation of antitrust enforcement in the 1980s has left labor and other Democratic constituencies with little protection against the threat to their interests posed by the largest wave of corporate reorganizations—hostile takeovers, leveraged buyouts, plant closings—since the days of J. P. Morgan.

Deregulation has also eroded the accommodations between business and labor that were fashioned by the Democrats. During the New Deal period, the federal government established or extended a regime of regulation over numerous sectors of the American economy. Characteristically, these regulations restricted price competition among firms within the regulated industry and, in some cases, erected barriers to the entry of new firms. To the extent that firms within such industries could pass added costs to their customers without fear of being undersold by competitors, they lost an incentive to control their labor costs. Union-management relations in most regulated industries were consequently more cooperative than adversarial in character. Rather than fight one another over wages and work rules, unions and employers entered the political arena as allies to defend and extend the regulatory regime and to secure direct or indirect public subsidies for their industries.

Asserting that these business-labor accommodations served "special interests" at the expense of the "public interest," an unlikely coalition of conservatives and liberal consumer advocates secured a substantial measure of deregulation during the late 1970s.[4] Through deregulation, conservatives hoped to get business to break its alliance with organized labor. Consumer advocates, for their part, were happy to weaken the labor unions and business interests that had been their rivals for influence within the Democratic party.

In the face of the threats that Reaganism posed to them both, liberals and labor rekindled their coalition in the 1980s. Increasingly, organized labor supported liberal causes, such as the nuclear freeze and comparable worth, that it would formerly have disdained. Liberals, for their part, have begun to see merit in a number of causes supported by organized labor, such as protectionism, and have lost their enthusiasm for deregulation.

The Republicans, though, have continued to press for deregulation, and with good reason. Particularly in airlines, telecommunications, and trucking, deregulation has allowed nonunion firms to undersell the established giants in their industry. Established firms have been compelled to demand give-backs from their unions to lower their own labor costs, and alliances between business and labor have been disrupted.

REORGANIZING POLITICAL FORCES

By undermining the governing capacities of institutions over which the Democrats exercise influence, the Republicans have also weakened the Democrats' social base. They have destabilized some of the major political forces upon which the Democrats depend and reoganized them under Republican auspices.

Most observers assume that politicians must deal with whatever groups they find in society, but it is important to note that political leaders are not limited to working with some predefined constellation of forces. At times, politicians can destroy established centers of power, reorganize interests, and even call new groups into being. Leaders can attempt to reorganize the constellation of interests central to the political process in several ways. They may be able to transform the political identities of established groups, create new political forces by dividing existing groups, or construct new interests by uniting previously disparate elements. In these ways, the Republicans have worked to reshape the political attachments of business executives, middle-class suburbanites, blue-collar ethnics, and white southerners.

Reunifying Business

Over the past fifteen years, the Republicans have undertaken to unify the business community under their auspices. After World War II, the Democrats had come to terms with many segments of big business—internationally competitive firms that benefited from free-trade policies, firms in

108

capital-intensive industries that found it relatively easy to make concessions to organized labor, and defense contractors who benefited from a foreign policy of internationalism.[5] However, proprietors of smaller firms that were not involved in international markets often found Democratic labor and social programs onerous, and they characteristically aligned themselves with the Republican party. This breach between Wall Street and Main Street undermined the political potency of American business.

During the 1970s, the accord between big business and the Democratic party was severely strained by two developments that the Republicans sought to exploit. The erosion of America's position in the world economy caused many business leaders to reject the high labor costs and taxes associated with the Democrats that they had previously accepted. And Democratic support for environmental, consumer, and other new regulatory programs further alienated many of the party's allies in the business community. In his 1980 presidential campaign, Ronald Reagan appealed for the support of business by indicating that he would trim costly social programs, weaken the influence of organized labor, and relax the environmental rules and other forms of regulation that had been sponsored by Democratic politicians during the 1960s and 1970s. Moreover, Reagan offered the thousands of firms that stood to benefit from military contracts substantial increases in defense spending.

Enacted into law, these policies helped to reunify American business and attach it to the Republican party.[6] This unity has since been threatened by the enormous budget and trade deficits that were generated by major tax cuts and military spending increases during Reagan's first term. The budget and trade deficits have produced a conflict between what may be termed the "traditionalist" and "supply-side" camps within the Republican party. The traditionalists assert that the nation's first economic priority must be to reduce the budget deficit—through budget cuts and, if necessary, tax increases. The supply-siders have been prepared to accept continuing deficits in order to protect tax cuts and to avoid reductions in defense spending.[7]

The conflict between traditionalists and supply-siders has two sources. The first is a difference in economic and political perspectives. Traditionalist Republicans fear that continuing huge deficits could wreck the economy, and hence their party's electoral fortunes. Supply-siders assert that the deficit poses no immediate threat to the economy, and they fear that steps taken to cut the deficit—such as raising taxes—could severely damage Republican electoral prospects.

The second source of disagreement between traditionalists and supply-siders is the conflict between two sets of economic interests in the Republican party. Large budget and trade deficits hurt sectors of the economy that produce goods in the United States for export (e.g., agriculture) and face competition in the American market from goods produced abroad (such as steel). Large budget deficits also exert upward pressure on interest rates, hurting local banks and thrift institutions. Together, these interests are the mainstays of the traditionalist camp.

Other sectors of American business (notably, domestic importers of goods produced by foreign manufacturers), however, have benefited from Republican economic policies. Firms in the service sector are not severely affected by interest rates or the trade deficit, but they have prospered as a result of the macroeconomic stimulus provided by budget deficits. At one time, the national banking and financial communities probably would have supported the traditionalists, but the banking industry is no longer as unified as it was in earlier Republican party battles. Banking deregulation and the development of new financial instruments, such as interest-rate and foreign-currency futures, enable large financial institutions to hedge against adverse interest- and exchange-rate fluctuations, thereby reducing their fear of government deficits. Although the financial community favors deficit reduction, the coexistence in the 1980s of huge deficits and booming financial markets suggests that this is not its only political priority.

In the battle for the 1988 Republican presidential nomination, George Bush was the leader of the supply-side forces and Senator Robert Dole spoke for the traditionalists. But once Bush wrapped up the nomination, all segments of the business community united behind his candidacy. However uneasy some business executives might have been over budget deficits, they were even more distrustful of a Democratic party whose leading representatives called for the enactment of plant-closing legislation, higher levels of social service spending, and increased taxes on the wealthy.

From Beneficiaries to Taxpayers

Middle-income suburbanites are a second group to which the Republicans appeal. The GOP has attempted to convince these voters to regard themselves less as beneficiaries of federal expenditure programs than as taxpayers.

After World War II, many suburbanites were integrated into the political process and linked to the Democratic party by federal programs that subsidized mortgages, built arterial highways, and expanded access to higher education. By placating the poor and reducing working-class militancy, Democratic welfare and labor programs also promoted social peace. In exchange for the benefits they received, members of the middle class gave their support to the various expenditure programs through which the Democratic party channeled public funds to its other constituency groups: crop subsidies for farmers, maritime subsidies for the shipping industry, and so on. This system of interest group liberalism enabled the Democrats to accommodate the claims of a host of disparate groups in their electoral coalition.[8]

During the 1960s and 1970s, many benefits that middle-income Americans had come to expect from federal programs and policies were sharply curtailed. For example, rising mortgage interest rates increased housing costs, affirmative action programs seemed to threaten the middle class's privileged access to higher education, social peace was disrupted by urban violence and riots, and, above all, double-digit inflation during the late 1970s eroded the middle class's real income and standard of living. The curtailment of these benefits undermined the political basis of the loyalty that many middle-income individuals had shown to the Democrats. This provided the GOP with an opportunity to win their support.[9]

In wooing suburbanites, the GOP has chosen not to promise new federal benefits although, to be sure, it has not sought to repeal existing middle-class benefit programs. Instead, the GOP has sought to link these individuals to the

Republican camp in their capacity as taxpayers. In 1980, Reagan declared tax relief to be a central political issue. The Republicans argued that taxation is linked to inflation and blamed high rates of inflation on Democratic tax and spending policies. Indeed, Reagan called inflation the "cruelest tax of all."

After Reagan's 1980 election, his administration cooperated with Federal Reserve Board Chairman Paul Volcker in a relentless attack on inflation.[10] The Reagan-Volcker war on inflation was successful, albeit at the cost of a severe recession and high rates of unemployment for blue-collar workers. At the same time, the Reagan administration provided middle- and upper-income groups with a sizeable reduction in federal income tax rates. Reagan's warning to middle-income voters that the Democrats wanted to take their tax cuts away was a crucial element of his successful 1984 campaign against Democratic presidential candidate Walter Mondale. This theme was echoed by George Bush in 1988. Bush promised to oppose any efforts to raise federal income tax rates and heaped scorn on Michael Dukakis's proposal to step up collection of delinquent federal taxes. Bush derided what he characterized as a Democratic plan to put an Internal Revenue Service auditor into every taxpayer's home.

The Republican party has successfully convinced middle-income Americans to focus on taxes. In 1976, only 2 percent of middle-class voters identified taxes and spending as important national problems; by 1984, 23 percent of voters with above-average incomes did so. Of these voters, 67 percent cast their ballots for the Republican presidential candidate.[11]

Republicans have appealed to members of the middle

class as taxpayers rather than as beneficiaries of spending programs chiefly because they hope to erode middle-income support for domestic expenditures in general. Transforming middle-class Americans into taxpayers not only links them to the Republican party but also helps to undermine the entire apparatus of interest group liberalism through which the Democrats have maintained their various constituencies' allegiances. This helps to disorganize the Democrats' political base.

Republican tax policies have also served to divide a politically important middle-class group—college-educated professionals—that had given substantial support to the Democrats during the 1960s and 1970s. Socially, this group is quite heterogeneous, ranging from ill-paid social workers to lavishly compensated attorneys. The group is so heterogeneous that sociologists have debated whether it is meaningful to speak of this "new class" as a coherent social and political force.[12] But groups are constituted in the political realm, and during the 1960s and 1970s political entrepreneurs were able to mobilize large numbers of professionals on behalf of such liberal causes as environmentalism and opposition to the Vietnam war.

The Republicans have attempted to divide this new class by shifting the political debate to the issues of tax and budget cuts. The 1981 tax cut was promoted as a means of stimulating the private sector. The tax reform package that Reagan made the centerpiece of his second administration was especially beneficial to professionals with high salaries. Professionals in a position to take advantage of these new opportunities—namely, those who work in the private sector—were attracted into the Republican party.

Republican reductions in federal domestic expenditures

have, however, restricted opportunities for professionals who work in the public and nonprofit sectors. The Republicans have not been altogether unhappy to see schoolteachers, social workers, and university professors try to defend their interests by becoming increasingly active in Democratic party politics. The more committed the Democrats become to the cause of boosting domestic expenditures, the more likely it is that taxpayers, business executives, and private-sector professionals will flock to the Republican party.

This Republican strategy has been quite successful. College graduates working in public-sector occupations gave the Republicans only 40 percent of their votes in the 1984 presidential election. On the other hand, college graduates in the private sector supported the GOP by the overwhelming margin of 68 percent to 32 percent for the Democrats. In terms of party identification, among college graduates in the public sector, Democrats outnumber Republicans 54 percent to 20 percent. By contrast, among private-sector college graduates, 40 percent identify with the Republican party and only 29 percent with the Democrats.

From Workers to Patriots

The GOP also now seeks to appeal to blue-collar voters. During the New Deal era, members of urban ethnic groups had been integrated into politics in their capacity as workers, through organizations informally affiliated with the national Democratic party—trade unions, political machines, and urban service bureaucracies. These institutions provided members of urban ethnic groups with public and

115

private employment at relatively high wages, with social services, and with preferential access to locally administered federal programs. At the same time, trade unions and urban machines and bureaucracies functioned as the local institutional foundations of the national Democratic party, mobilizing urban voters to support Democratic candidates.[13]

The Republicans have weakened the links between the Democrats and blue-collar workers by attacking these institutions. They have undermined organized labor by encouraging employers to engage in antiunion practices; indeed, the Reagan administration set an example by destroying the Professional Air Traffic Controllers Organization when the group conducted a strike in 1981.[14] The Republicans have also appointed officials who are hostile to organized labor to the National Labor Relations Board (an agency formerly controlled by labor sympathizers). Moreover, as discussed above, the Reagan and Bush administrations have supported policies of deregulation that provide business firms with a strong incentive to rid themselves of their unions. The Republican commitment to free trade also allows foreign goods to flood American markets, increasing unemployment in heavily unionized industries and reducing labor's bargaining power. As a result of these policies, union membership dropped sharply during the 1980s (see figure 4.2).

The Republicans have attacked urban political machines and national and municipal service bureaucracies mainly through domestic spending reductions. The programs whose budgets have suffered most under Reagan and Bush are precisely those that once provided local governments with substantial funds, such as revenue sharing and the Comprehensive Employment and Training Act (CETA).

116

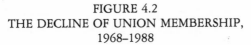

FIGURE 4.2
THE DECLINE OF UNION MEMBERSHIP,
1968–1988

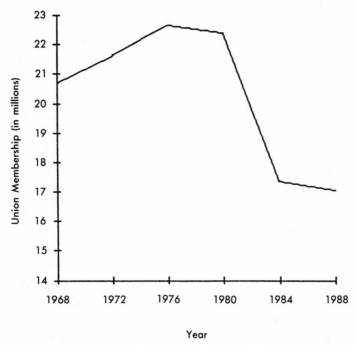

SOURCE: 1968–1979, U.S. Department of Labor, Bureau of Labor Statistics, *Directory of National Unions and Employee Associations, 1979. Bulletin 2079* (Washington, D.C.: U.S. Government Printing Office, 1980); 1980–1988, U.S. Department of Labor, Bureau of Labor Statistics, *Employment and Earnings* (Washington, D.C.: U.S. Government Printing Office, 1989).

The tax reform package whose enactment was secured by the Reagan administration in 1986 reduced the deductability of local sales taxes (thereby heightening taxpayers' resistance to rate increases) and restricted the ability of local governments to issue tax-free revenue bonds. These changes in the tax code further diminish the resources avail-

117

able to municipal governments. The Justice Department has also attacked urban machines and bureaucracies by launching a series of investigations into municipal government corruption; these investigations have been primarily targeted at large cities controlled by the Democrats.[15]

The attack on labor unions, political machines, and social service agencies diminishes the ability of these institutions to provide benefits to blue-collar voters; thus, this group's links to the Democratic party have been undermined, and Republicans have an opportunity to capture the support of a previously staunch Democratic constituency.

The Republicans' appeal to this constituency has been hindered in one important way. In their capacity as workers, many urban ethnic voters have been hurt by Republican economic and tax programs, which mainly serve the interests of the upper middle class and segments of the business community. Instead of trying to appeal to members of urban ethnic groups on economic grounds, therefore, the Republicans have attempted to secure and institutionalize their support on three other bases. First, they have sought to link urban ethnics to the GOP on the basis of their moral and religious convictions. The Republicans have politicized these concerns by focusing on so-called family issues—above all, the issue of abortion. In this endeavor, they have sought to make use of Roman Catholic churches, which rally the faithful against pro-abortion candidates.[16] The importance of this political focus became evident during the 1984 presidential election. White working-class voters who belonged to trade unions but did not regularly attend a church gave Reagan only 46 percent of their vote. By contrast, among white working-class voters who attended a church regularly but did not belong to a union, the Republicans received 67 percent of the vote.

The Republicans have attempted to mobilize blue-collar voters with patriotic as well as moral appeals. In this effort they have at times been able to harness the national media—an institution whose editorial pages and televised commentary frequently have been hostile to Republican policies. As discussed in chapter 1, Reagan and Bush have created news events filled with patriotic symbols that the media can neither attack nor ignore. In addition, where the risks of failure are low, Republican administrations have used military force abroad not only to demonstrate America's resolve to foreigners but also to reinforce national pride among Americans. The 1984 Grenada invasion and the 1986 bombing of Libya exemplify this strategy. During the 1988 presidential campaign, Bush sought to make political use of patriotic sentiments by charging that his Democratic rival, Massachusetts Governor Michael Dukakis, had demonstrated a lack of respect for the American flag when he vetoed a Massachusetts bill that mandated the daily recitation of the pledge of allegiance in public schools.

Finally, the Republicans have made use of race-related issues to seek support from blue-collar whites. The Reagan and Bush administrations have opposed affirmative action and school busing plans and have promoted efforts to narrow the rights that the liberal Warren Court had granted to persons accused of crimes. In his 1988 presidential campaign, Bush made a major issue of the Willie Horton case. Horton, a black man, had been convicted of murder and sentenced to life imprisonment without parole. Under a program supported by Governor Michael Dukakis, Massa-

119

chusetts prison authorities granted Horton a weekend furlough. While on furlough, Horton fled the state and raped
a white woman in Maryland. Groups supporting the Bush
campaign repeatedly broadcast television ads displaying a
picture of Horton and asserting that Dukakis was soft on
crime.

From Southerners to Evangelicals

Southern whites are the fourth constituency that the
Republicans strive to add to their camp. For a century after
the Civil War, white southerners had participated in politics
through the Democratic party, which had defended the
southern caste system. These voters were linked to the
Democrats not simply by their racial attitudes, but also by
local political institutions that were connected with the
party—county commissions, sheriffs, voting registrars—and
that guaranteed white political power by excluding blacks
from participation in government and politics.[17]

The civil rights revolution—in particular, the Voting
Rights Act of 1965—destroyed the institutional foundations of the traditional southern Democratic regime. Local
governmental institutions were prevented from maintaining white privilege at the expense of black political subordination. The disruption of this system gave Republicans an
opportunity to win the support of southern whites. The
GOP stance on affirmative action, busing, and the rights of
defendants in criminal trials has helped them to win support
among white southerners as well as northern blue-collar
voters. The GOP has also appealed to southerners on the
basis of their religious orientations. By focusing on the issue

of abortion, Republicans have politicized the moral concerns of white southerners. They have made use of fundamentalist Protestant churches, a prominent feature of the southern landscape, to forge institutional links between southern whites and the Republican party. Republicans have in effect made these churches organizational components of their party. For example, funds and technical support are provided to conservative Protestant churches for voter registration activities.

As a result of these efforts, many southern whites have been integrated into politics through their evangelical religious affiliations. This has helped to give the Republicans a firm social base in the white South for the first time in the party's 130-year history. In 1984, Ronald Reagan received 78 percent of the white fundamentalist and evangelical Christian vote. In 1988, an even larger proportion of these voters—81 percent—supported George Bush.[18]

As in the case of urban ethnics, who are mainly Roman Catholic, the moral issue that Republicans have used most effectively to appeal to white southerners is the issue of abortion. Indeed, Republicans have used the question of abortion to promote an alliance between evangelical southern Protestants and conservative Catholics and to attach both to the Republican party. Political mobilization around the right-to-life issue was initiated by Richard Vigurie, Paul Weyrich, Howard Phillips, and other conservative Republican activists. Seeking to take advantage of the furor caused by the Supreme Court's pro-choice decision in *Roe* v. *Wade,* these politicians convinced Catholic political activists and evangelical Protestant leaders that they had common interests and worked with these leaders to arouse public opposition to abortion. The right-to-life issue helped to politically unite, under Republican auspices, two religious groups that had been bitter opponents through much of American history.[19]

The Republicans have also used foreign policy and military issues to mobilize support among southerners. Military bases and defense plants play a major role in the economy of many southern states. Republican support and Democratic opposition to a military buildup during the 1980s tied many southern workers, business executives, and local communities to the GOP. Defense spending is thus the material foundation for the GOP's patriotic appeals that so successfully woo support in the white South. Almost none of the several dozen military installations that were closed (as a cost-cutting measure) in 1989 were located in the South; hence, that region's stake in defense spending will continue.[20]

CONSTRUCTING MECHANISMS OF GOVERNANCE

While the Democrats have entrenched themselves primarily in the social service and regulatory agencies of the domestic state, the Republicans have relied more heavily on two other mechanisms of governance. These are the military and national security apparatus, and monetary and fiscal policy.

The National Security Apparatus

The Republicans have worked since the early 1980s to increase the size and power of America's military and national security apparatus and to use it as an instrument for governing and perpetuating the power of the GOP. The Reagan administration sponsored the largest peacetime military buildup in the nation's history. As figure 4.3 indicates, military expenditures in constant dollars increased from $171 billion per year at the end of the Carter administration to $242 billion by the middle of Reagan's second

FIGURE 4.3
GROWTH OF MILITARY SPENDING, 1979–1989*

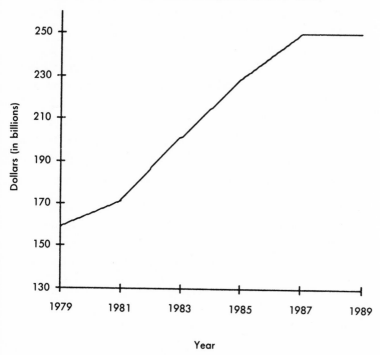

SOURCE: Office of Management and Budget, *Budget of the United States Government, Fiscal Year 1990, Historical Tables* (Washington, D.C.: U.S. Government Printing Office, 1989), table 6–1.
*Expenditures are in constant 1982 dollars.

123

presidential term. Subsequently, congressional opposition limited further increases in military spending to the annual rate of inflation. But the enormous military buildup of the first Reagan administration has enlarged the base upon which changes in military spending are now calculated.

When they controlled the White House, Democratic administrations had initiated domestic spending programs that solidified the party's ties to its numerous constituency groups. Such expenditures stimulated economic growth and employment, thereby identifying the Democrats as the party of prosperity. Thus, even interest groups that were not direct recipients of federal spending were given reason to support the Democrats. Republicans profess to reject the economic theory associated with Democratic spending programs, but have in effect adopted a program of military Keynesianism. Republican military programs have directly benefited segments of the business community, regions of the country, and elements of the electorate whose fortunes are tied to the military sector. At the same time, the economic growth, high levels of employment, and healthy corporate profits promoted by these programs provide Americans in general with reasons to support the GOP.

Republicans have also sought to develop a military version of the industrial policy often espoused by the Democrats. Under Democratic variants of industrial policy, decisions on the allocation of capital and the organization of production that now are the prerogative of business would involve union and public influence as well. The Republicans, by contrast, hope to enhance the competitiveness of American industry through means that reinforce rather than limit the prerogatives of corporate management. The

124

Reagan-Bush military buildup has been central to this endeavor. Republican military programs have emphasized producing and procuring new weapons systems rather than bolstering personnel or enhancing readiness and maintenance. The purchase of new weapons provides subsidies to business and promotes the development of new technologies that may increase the strength and competitiveness of American industry. The Strategic Defense Initiative (SDI), or "Star Wars," is the most ambitious effort in this regard. As liberal economist Robert Reich has noted, the SDI program "could create whole new generations of telecommunications and computer-related products that could underpin information-processing systems in the next century."[21] This increase in American industrial competitiveness, it should be noted, would be achieved without infringing on the power of corporate executives.

The Republicans have also striven to use military programs as a form of social policy. They have worked to drastically slash domestic social spending but have been less hostile to the health, education, and income maintenance programs administered by the Veterans Administration (VA). Indeed, during Reagan's last year in office, the VA was elevated to a cabinet-level department. The programs administered by this department are identical to domestic welfare programs in all respects but one—historically, they have been linked to conservative veterans' organizations rather than to liberal political forces. Under the rubric of putting an end to waste, fraud, and abuse, the Republicans thus have slashed the welfare programs that were politically beneficial to their opponents, while funding programs that serve their political friends. Conservative veterans' groups, for their part, have been more than willing to endorse Republican military ventures and lobby on behalf of GOP foreign policies.

Monetary and Fiscal Policy

The complex of Republican policies described in this chapter is sustained by a fiscal regime that is one of the most notable features of the contemporary American political economy.[22] Central to this regime are the enormous budget and trade deficits of the Reagan-Bush years. The budget deficit resulted from the tax reductions and military spending increases of the first Reagan administration and from Congress's opposition to further domestic spending cuts. In conjunction with the restrictive monetary policies the Federal Reserve pursued in its fight against inflation, the budget deficit led to sharp increases in real interest rates and the value of the American dollar in the early 1980s. These increases greatly reduced American exports and encouraged a flood of foreign imports into the United States. During the second Reagan administration, coordinated central bank intervention led the dollar to fall, but by this time foreign manufacturers had established such a solid position in the American market that the nation's trade deficit continued to grow. As figure 4.4 indicates, the U.S. balance of trade, which had been positive from World War II through the 1960s, reached a deficit of approximately $150 billion in the 1986–87 period. This deficit declined to roughly $130 billion in 1988.

Despite the economic risks they pose, these deficits provide the Republicans with important political benefits and

126

FIGURE 4.4
AMERICA'S GROWING MERCHANDISE TRADE
DEFICIT, 1978–1988

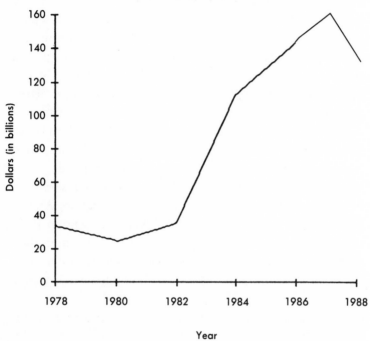

SOURCE: *The Economic Report of the President* (Washington, D.C.: U.S. Government
Printing Office, 1988), 364.

opportunities. The budget deficit makes it difficult for
politicians to appeal for votes with new public expenditure
programs and impedes the Democrats' efforts to recon-
struct their political base. More importantly, the twin deficits function as a novel revenue-collection apparatus that, at
least in the short run, enables the Republicans to finance
government expenditures without raising taxes and alienating their political constituency.

127

This apparatus works as follows. The Reagan administration's fiscal policies encouraged Americans to purchase foreign—especially Japanese and German—goods. At the same time, America's high interest rates and political stability have encouraged foreign bankers—most notably the Japanese—to purchase U.S. Treasury securities with the profits their nation's manufacturers make in the United States. Thus, during the 1980s, what might be called "autodollars" came to be recycled by Japanese banks, much as "petrodollars" were recycled by American banks in the 1970s. These autodollars, invested in U.S. government securities, have been used to help finance the American budget deficit.[23] In essence, Japanese industrialists and bankers have served as revenue agents for the Republican administration. American voters demonstrated in 1980, 1984, and again in 1988 that they opposed increased taxation, but as consumers they willingly—indeed, enthusiastically—hand over billions of dollars for this purpose whenever they purchase Japanese and other foreign-made goods.

The costs of this revenue system are borne by unemployed American workers in the industrial sector and by American manufacturers who fail to restructure their firms to meet foreign competition. The benefits of the system flow to groups with which the Republicans are allied. Military spending benefits the defense industry and its thousands of subcontractors. The fiscal stimulus of the deficit boosts corporate profits. High-income professionals have received substantial tax cuts, access to foreign goods at low prices, and high rates of return on their savings.

This fiscal regime came under attack during the late 1980s and the White House has been compelled to accept some adjustments to it. Nevertheless, it remains central to the structure of extraction and distribution prevailing in the United States today; this revenue system accounts for perhaps one-third of the federal government's discretionary spending. It is thus a key component of the political and governmental system that the Republicans constructed in the 1980s.

Taken together, the fiscal, monetary, and national security policies of the Reagan and Bush administrations have strengthened the institutional bastions and governing capacities of the Republicans and threatened those of the Democrats. This Republican offensive and the Democrats' response initiated the institutional conflicts that are at the heart of American politics today.

5

Institutional Combat

As the Democratic and Republican parties have developed bastions in different institutions and sectors of American government, the character of American politics has been transformed. Intense institutional struggles have increasingly come to supplant electoral competition as the central focus of politics in the United States. Conflicts over the budget and trade deficits, foreign and defense policy, and judicial power that have raged during the Reagan and Bush years can only be understood in light of these struggles.

DEFICITS AND INSTITUTIONAL COMBAT

The budget and tax cuts enacted during the Reagan presidency, as we have seen, have been crucial to the Republican party's effort to expand its own influence and weaken political forces and governmental institutions controlled by its opponents. These spending cuts have diminished the flow of resources to groups and forces with close ties to the

131

Democrats. The tax cuts have generated enormous budget and trade deficits. The economic dislocations caused by these deficits have weakened two other institutions linked to the Democrats—labor unions in import-sensitive industries and municipal governments in the nation's industrial belt.

Equally important, the Reagan tax cuts have served to restrict the distributive and extractive capacities of Congress. The enormous budget deficits resulting from the 1981 tax cuts limit Congress's ability to enact new spending programs, because such programs would further exacerbate the deficit problem. And the 1986 tax reform act has reduced the extractive capacities of Congress, by eliminating many of the exemptions, deductions, and preferences that in prior decades had made high nominal tax rates politically acceptable.

The Republicans' attack on Congress and other institutions affiliated with the Democrats was initially quite successful. Congress was unable to enact a single major new domestic spending program during the first six years of Reagan's presidency. After the Democrats regained control of the Senate in 1987, some new legislation was enacted, but Congress was able to establish only programs that imposed no additional burdens on the U.S. Treasury. For example, the costs of the 1988 statute requiring employers to provide prior notification of plant closings fell upon private business firms rather than the federal government. And the catastrophic health care legislation enacted in 1988 was financed by premium increases and surcharges borne by Medicare recipients, rather than new budgetary outlays.

Deadlock between Congress and the president over

methods of coping with the deficit has reduced Congress's ability to play a leading role in macroeconomic management.[1] The deadlock prevents fiscal policy—over which Congress exercises ultimate authority—from being adjusted in light of changing economic conditions and greatly increases the significance of monetary and exchange-rate policies. These policies are controlled by agencies that are directly or indirectly subject to administration influence—the Federal Reserve and the Treasury Department. With White House support, the Federal Reserve squeezed inflation from the economy by raising real interest rates (see figure 5.1). High real interest rates also helped attract the huge foreign purchases of U.S. government securities that are necessary to fund the budget deficit.

During the mid-1980s, congressional Democrats mounted a two-pronged assault on this Republican fiscal system by attacking the budget and trade deficits. Congressional Democrats and Republicans unhappy with the budget deficit united in December 1985 to secure the enactment of the Gramm-Rudman-Hollings deficit reduction act. The act set deficit targets for balancing the budget over a period of five years and mandated across-the-board cuts in defense and domestic programs if the targets were not met. Calculating that the president would not willingly reduce military spending, the Democrats saw Gramm-Rudman-Hollings as a way to compel him to accept tax increases. Republicans who were concerned with the adverse impact of the deficit on key sectors of the economy (traditionalists, as we have named them) were prepared to accept either tax increases or spending cuts to reduce the budget deficit. Some Republicans, including Senator Phil Gramm, sup-

FIGURE 5.1
REAL INTEREST RATES, 1967–1987*

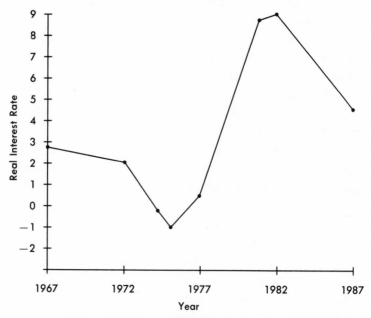

SOURCE: *The Economic Report of the President* (Washington, D.C.: U.S. Government Printing Office, 1988), 317, 330.
*The real interest rate is the difference between the average prime rate and the annual percentage change in the consumer price index.

ported the bill as a way to compel Congress to accept further domestic spending cuts and prevent their political opponents from capitalizing on the deficit issue.

The second weapon the Democrats deployed against the Republican fiscal system was protectionism. By blocking the flow of foreign imports into the United States, the Democrats hoped to protect the jobs of workers in heavily unionized manufacturing industries.[2] Protectionism would also reduce foreign purchases of U.S. Treasury securities and limit the administration's ability to rely on this means of funding the budget deficit.

The administration responded to this threat by joining the nation's major trading partners (Japan, Germany, Great Britain, and France, the four other members of the so-called Group of Five) in the Plaza agreement of September 1985. In an effort to stimulate American exports, the Group of Five undertook to drive down the value of the American dollar. Over the next two years the dollar fell by nearly one-half against both the Japanese yen and the German mark, but the United States continued to run an enormous trade deficit. Moreover, the declining dollar threatened to revive domestic inflation, and America's foreign creditors were appalled to see the value of their holdings in dollar-denominated securities shrink.[3]

As the value of the dollar continued to fall, foreign private investors became reluctant to purchase additional U.S. Treasury notes and bonds; their reluctance threatened the administration's ability to fund the American budget deficit. Therefore, in the Louvre Accords of 1987, the United States and the other leading industrial nations agreed to stabilize the value of the dollar. Japan and Germany agreed to reduce their interest rates and pursue expansionary fiscal policies. The United States promised to raise its interest rates and reduce its budget deficits—thus strengthening the dollar. They hoped that these coordinated policies would improve the U.S. trade deficit by increasing the market for American goods in Germany and Japan, while reducing German and Japanese exports to the United States.[4]

Following the Louvre accords, the United States did increase its interest rates. However, disagreements emerged over the extent to which the major participants had fulfilled

135

their other commitments. The Germans and Japanese asserted that the Americans had not sufficiently reduced the U.S. budget deficit, whereas the Americans claimed that the other two, especially Germany, had not sufficiently stimulated their domestic economies.

In the fall of 1987, rising interest rates and the U.S. trade deficit's failure to improve weakened the American stock market. Investor confidence was also shaken by the continuing conflict between the United States and its trading partners over implementation of the Louvre accords. This conflict came to a head in mid-October when Treasury Secretary James Baker threatened to allow the dollar to resume its fall unless Germany cut its interest rates. Investors feared that a further decline in the value of the dollar would prompt foreigners to abandon the American stock and bond markets. These fears sparked the stock market collapse of October 19, 1987.

In the wake of the crash, both the administration and Congress came under increased pressure to reduce the budget deficit. However, the White House remained firmly opposed to significant tax increases or cuts in military spending, and congressional Democrats opposed any substantial cuts in domestic spending. Negotiations between the White House and Congress following the crash thus produced little more than token deficit reductions.

The Bush administration's budget negotiations with Congress in 1989 made it clear that Bush, like Reagan, is reluctant to accept the tax increases that are a political and economic precondition for reducing the deficit. Like its predecessor, the Bush administration proposed meeting the requirements of the Gramm-Rudman Act by optimistically forecasting that economic growth and declining interest rates would reduce the deficit without any major increases in revenues or reductions in spending. These optimistic forecasts are no more likely to pan out in the 1990s than they were in the 1980s. It appears that Bush, like Reagan, is prepared to tolerate deficits.

Despite all that has transpired in the past decade, congressional Democrats have been unable to destroy the Republican fiscal regime, whose foundations were laid by the 1981 tax cuts. Tax receipts continue to run well behind government spending, large deficits endure, and imported

FIGURE 5.2
FOREIGN HOLDINGS OF U.S. TREASURY
SECURITIES

SOURCE: *The Economic Report of the President* (Washington, D.C.: U.S. Government Printing Office, 1983, 1988), 281, 369.

goods continue to flood American markets. As figure 5.2 illustrates, foreign funds have played and continue to play a major role in financing the American budget deficit.

Struggles over fiscal policy have been prominent in American politics in recent years because the deficit has become a central determinant of the relative power of Congress and the presidency—and of the political forces linked to each. The persistence of large deficits indicates that, in this arena of institutional combat, the Republicans retain the upper hand.

THE NATIONAL SECURITY APPARATUS AND INSTITUTIONAL COMBAT

Just as they have sought to make political use of fiscal policy, the Republicans in recent decades have used the military and national security apparatus as a political weapon.

After World War II, there had been a bipartisan consensus in the United States on questions of foreign and military policy.[5] Democrats and Republicans agreed on the need to maintain powerful military forces and a capacity for covert intelligence operations. The leaders of both parties were prepared to deploy these forces to contain the Soviet Union and its allies and to fight left-wing insurgent movements. The Vietnam War destroyed this consensus. Antiwar forces gained influence within the Democratic party and were able to impose limits on both military expenditures and American intervention in Third World conflicts. Reagan Republicans regarded Democratic "neo-isolationism" as a danger to the nation—and as an opportunity for their party's political gain.

The Reagan defense buildup of the 1980s has attached social forces with a stake in defense programs to the GOP, and it has created a governing apparatus that supplants institutions of the domestic state linked to the Democrats. Thus, as noted earlier, the Reagan administration adopted policies of military Keynesianism to stimulate the economy, used military procurement as a form of industrial policy, and maintained funding for VA social programs while attempting to drastically slash spending on welfare programs administered by domestic agencies. Reagan and Bush have also sought to reassert their prerogative to deploy American military force abroad, to conduct covert intelligence operations, and to support guerrilla movements fighting Soviet-backed regimes. Thus, without seeking the prior approval of Congress, the Reagan administration sent troops to invade Grenada and aircraft to bomb Libya. American ground troops were sent to intervene in Lebanon in 1982 and American naval forces were sent into action in the Persian Gulf in 1988. Large quantities of American arms were supplied to pro-Western forces in Angola and Afghanistan. The Reagan administration rebuilt the CIA's capacity to engage in covert operations by greatly expanding its budget and personnel and by attempting to circumvent congressional scrutiny of intelligence operations, particularly in Central America where the White House hoped to undermine the Sandinista regime in Nicaragua.

The Reagan and Bush administrations have also made efforts to develop alliances with foreign governments that could help them to achieve political goals that would be unattainable through America's own governmental institutions. The most important of these alliances has been a tacit one with the government of Japan. Despite protectionist pressures, the White House has largely kept America's borders open to a flood of Japanese goods. In turn, the Japanese government helps fund the American budget deficit by purchasing U.S. Treasury securities through its central bank and by encouraging private Japanese financial institutions to do the same. This alliance with Japan has permitted both the Reagan and Bush administrations to maintain high levels of military spending without raising taxes.

The White House has also entered into joint ventures with the leaders of Israel and Saudi Arabia. The Reagan administration and the Israelis cooperated in channeling arms to Iran. The administration also sold advanced weapons to Saudi Arabia, and the Saudi royal family helped finance the Nicaraguan Contra forces. In both instances, arrangements with a foreign government were used by the White House to circumvent congressional opposition.

A number of these Republican ventures were quite successful. President Reagan oversaw the largest peacetime military buildup in the nation's history. Military spending has provided major segments of industry and regions of the country with a continuing stake in the success of the Republicans and has helped fuel the longest period of economic expansion in the postwar period. Reagan also demonstrated that it was possible, despite the trauma of Vietnam, for a politician to increase his popularity at home by using American forces abroad.

Congressional Democrats have sought to block the Republicans' use of the national security apparatus as a political weapon. Liberal Democrats resisted the president's military buildup, arguing that Reaganite military policies, especially SDI, would provoke an arms race with the Soviets and serve more to diminish than to enhance American security. Democrats asserted that the nation's security would be better served by arms control agreements, and they demanded that the administration pursue serious negotiations with the Soviet Union to achieve reductions in nuclear and conventional forces. To this end, Democrats gave their support to what became the largest peace movement since the end of the Vietnam War and to its key proposal—the nuclear freeze.[6] Though the freeze proposal ultimately failed, arms control was a central issue for the Democrats throughout the course of the Reagan administration. Arms control also promised to reduce the Republicans' ability to derive political benefits from military spending and to make more money available for domestic programs.

Not long after the defeat of the nuclear freeze proposal, congressional Democrats found a new way to attack the Republican military buildup. They charged that waste and fraud were rampant in the military procurement process and suggested that much of the money being appropriated for defense was actually lining the pockets of unscrupulous defense contractors.[7] In televised testimony, witnesses displayed toilet seats, coffee pots, and hammers for which defense contractors had billed the American taxpayer hundreds or even thousands of dollars.[8] This attack was equivalent to the conservatives' crusades against welfare fraud— an effort to discredit a major spending program by focusing on the abuses that inevitably accompany it. The campaign against waste and fraud in military procurement helped undermine support for the Reagan buildup and, with the pressure of the growing federal budget deficit, permitted Congress to hold defense spending increases to the rate of

141

inflation after Reagan's first term. The Democrats continued their attack on military spending during the Bush presidency, forcing cutbacks in costly weapons systems, such as the B-2 "Stealth" bomber.

In addition to attacking the administration's military buildup, liberal Democrats sought to turn veterans' programs to their own political advantage. Liberals created organizations of Vietnam veterans that were separate from the leading veterans' groups, the American Legion and the Veterans of Foreign Wars. Traditional veterans' groups serve the conservative cause by extolling the American military and supporting a strong defense; the new Vietnam veterans' groups portray soldiers who served in Southeast Asia as victims of American military policy. Rather than glorify the American military establishment, they emphasize the suffering the military imposed even on its own soldiers—for example, by exposing them to the toxic herbicide Agent Orange. These liberal veterans' groups have also sought to gain access to the resources of the Department of Veterans Affairs, for example, by demanding that it fund programs for the treatment of "post-traumatic stress disorder," a condition they assert is common among Vietnam veterans.[9]

Congressional Democrats worked to block Reagan's efforts to deploy military forces abroad and to further his policy goals through U.S. alliances with foreign governments. Reagan's opponents tried to compel him to end U.S. military involvement in Lebanon and criticized him for failing to use the procedures outlined in the War Powers Act to secure congressional approval for the deployment of American forces in the Persian Gulf.[10] Moreover, congressional Democrats attacked the administration's alliances with foreign dictators. For example, Congress played a key role in the sequence of events that led to the ouster of Philippine dictator Ferdinand Marcos, an ally of successive American administrations. As noted above, the administration's opponents also used protectionism to attack the alliance with Japan upon which the Republican fiscal regime depends.

Finally, congressional Democrats attacked the administration's Nicaragua policy by compelling the CIA to stop mining harbors, insisting that the agency withdraw a training manual that advocated the assassination of Sandinista cadres, and by publicizing charges that the Contras were engaged in drug smuggling and routinely violated human rights. The Democrats ultimately were able to restrict Reagan's aid to the contras by enacting a series of amendments—the Boland amendments—to foreign military assistance bills.

The Iran-Contra Affair

In the face of congressional Democratic opposition to administration policy in Nicaragua, conservative forces within the Reagan administration built an alternative intelligence apparatus attached to the National Security Council. This apparatus enabled them to conduct covert operations (such as aid to the Contras) that Congress had refused to approve, as well as activities (such as the sale of weapons to Iran) that Congress would certainly not countenance.

The network was managed by CIA director William Casey, marine colonel Oliver North, and retired Air Force general Richard Secord. When the network was discovered, critics in Congress called it a "state within the state." The characterization is not inappropriate; that covert system had some of the administrative, extractive, and coercive capacities of a governmental intelligence agency. The network was able to conduct covert operations because it was staffed by retired military officers and CIA operatives and had ties to foreign intelligence officials and arms merchants. Lacking access to tax revenues, the network was financed by gifts from foreign governments, contributions from wealthy American conservatives, and the profits from weapons sales to Iran. Depending on how one chooses to characterize its relationship with the anti-Sandinista forces—to which it provided political and military guidance as well as financial support—the network might be said to have had coercive capacities as well.[11]

The existence of the covert network was revealed at the end of 1986 in what came to be called the "Iran-contra affair." The eruption of the Iran-contra scandal did more than destroy this intelligence network. It disrupted and embarrassed the entire Reagan administration and strengthened institutions that compete with the presidency. The difficulties the administration experienced cannot simply be attributed to its committing a major blunder in selling arms to Iran in exchange for the release of American hostages and diverting some of the proceeds from those sales to the Contras. Scandals such as the Iran-contra affair must be understood as political events. Politically damaging revelations are a *consequence* of investigators' efforts to uncover facts that will embarrass an administration politically, as much as they are a *source* of that administration's difficulties. After all, prior to November 1986 there were press reports that Israel was shipping arms to Iran and that Oliver North was helping the Contras secure weapons, but neither the media nor Congress tried to discover the source of these arms. To account for the challenge that the Iran-contra affair posed to the Reagan presidency, one must look to changes within political constituencies and to institutional factors.

As for changes within political constituencies, two developments weakened the coalition Reagan had constructed and energized the institutions through which his opponents operated. First, the Democrats regained control of the U.S. Senate in the midterm elections of 1986. (The great benefits of incumbency in House elections had helped the Democrats to retain control of that chamber despite the GOP landslides in the 1980 and 1984 presidential elections.) The Democrats' success in 1986 emboldened the president's opponents in Congress. Their success also emboldened the press, which until then had treated the Reagan administration quite gingerly for fear of alienating its middle-class audience.

The second development that contributed to the administration's rapid loss of support as the Iran-contra affair unfolded was the emergence of a rift between the White House and elements of the nation's foreign policy establishment. Many members of that establishment were upset by the White House's behavior during and after the October 1986 Reykjavik summit—actions that had strained the Atlantic alliance. Foreign policy elites were appalled by revelations of the extent to which the White House had conducted sensitive operations in the Mideast and Central America through the Casey-North-Secord network. They

145

denounced the "cowboys" in the White House for constructing this covert network, supported the State Department's virtual declaration of independence after the Iran-contra scandal erupted, and joined in the attack on the Reagan administration.[12]

The Reagan administration was also weakened by the very way in which the Iranian weapons deal was conducted. The administration used a covert network of retired military officers and arms merchants to deal with Iran because its policy was opposed by the State and Defense Departments and would certainly have provoked a hostile reaction in Congress. The expedient of using this network was ultimately self-defeating, however, because after the weapons deal was revealed and the president came under attack, that network was not powerful enough to sustain him. Reagan could neither rely on it to maintain his Iranian initiative (which he continued to insist was a good idea), nor was that network linked to powerful social forces to which he could turn for political support.

The administration's opponents, by contrast, were able to use the formidable iron triangle of institutions—Congress, the national news media, and the federal judiciary—that had triumphed over the White House in the Watergate affair. The extent to which this nexus has become institutionalized is striking: After the diversion of funds to the Contras was revealed, it was universally assumed that Congress should conduct televised hearings and the judiciary should appoint an independent counsel to investigate and prosecute the officials involved in the episode. In contrast to President Nixon, Ronald Reagan recognized that it would be fruitless to assert claims of executive privilege, and he turned over all documents requested by the congressional investigators, including his personal diaries.

Nevertheless, in the Iran-contra investigation, Congress did not score as complete a victory over the White House as it had in the Watergate affair. Following the precedent of Watergate, congressional Democrats searched for evidence of direct presidential involvement in criminal activity—a "smoking gun." They thus focused the hearings on the illegal diversion of funds to the Contras more than on the sale of weapons to Iran. Their tactic, however, ultimately blunted the impact of the entire congressional investigation.

In his televised testimony, Colonel North skillfully portrayed the Contras as freedom fighters and generated far more public sympathy for his actions than would have been possible if he had been compelled to defend the sale of weapons to Ayatollah Khomeini's government. The outpouring of public support for North intimidated the Democrats and encouraged Republicans on the committee to depict the entire investigation as an exercise in partisan politics.[13] When North's superior, former National Security Adviser John Poindexter, asserted that he had neither informed the president of, nor secured presidential approval for, the fund diversion, the force of the congressional investigation was dissipated.

The blunting of the congressional investigation reduced the effectiveness of the probe conducted by independent counsel Lawrence Walsh. In the Watergate case, it was Congress that uncovered the key sources of evidence—the White House tapes—and stood ready to impeach President Nixon if he failed to turn these over to special prosecutor

Archibald Cox. In the Iran-contra case, Congress provided no such help to the independent counsel, and the administration was able to refuse to release many classified documents for use at North's trial.

The Reagan administration was not destroyed by Congress in the Iran-contra embroglio as the Nixon administration had been in the Watergate affair. Nevertheless, it was weakened. Reagan was compelled to appoint a national security adviser, a director of central intelligence, and a White House chief of staff acceptable to the opposition in Congress. Reagan was also compelled to appoint a presidential panel, the Tower Commission, to look into White House management of foreign affairs and to endure a good deal of ridicule when the commission issued a final report describing his rather lackadaisical "management style."

In the wake of the Iran-contra affair, Reagan also was unable to advance his conservative agenda any further. Indeed, he only found it possible to take major initiatives—most notably, in arms control—when these coincided with the agenda of his liberal opponents. The Reagan administration's negotiations with the Soviets did lead to the signing of a significant arms control agreement, the 1988 treaty banning intermediate-range nuclear missiles in Europe. Ironically, this foreign policy success restored Reagan's personal popularity and contributed to Bush's Republican victory in the 1988 presidential election.[14] Though the Republicans were able to overcome the potential electoral damage of the Iran-contra affair, it did end their use of the National Security Council to circumvent congressional influence over foreign policy. However, because of the limited scope of Congress's victory, Republican efforts to use defense and foreign policy agencies as institutions of governance have continued.

THE COURTS AND INSTITUTIONAL COMBAT

The federal judiciary has become another major focus of institutional conflict in contemporary American politics. During the past two decades, congressional Democrats and the White House have been locked in a struggle over both the scope of judicial power and who will control the courts. But the judiciary is not only an object of institutional struggles; it also has become a major participant in them.

An alliance between the federal courts and liberal political forces emerged during the postwar decades.[15] The judiciary took up causes of concern to liberals, most importantly, the defense of civil rights and civil liberties. Liberals, for their part, supported the federal judiciary's efforts to expand its jurisdiction, and they defended it when it came under attack by conservatives. This helped the courts substantially expand their role and power.

Since the 1960s, the Supreme Court has relaxed the rules governing justiciability—the conditions under which courts will hear a case—to greatly increase the range of issues with which the federal judiciary can deal. For example, the Court has liberalized the doctrine of standing to permit taxpayers' suits where First Amendment issues are involved. The Court has amended the Federal Rules of Civil Procedure to facilitate class-action suits. Claims that might have been rejected as *de minimis* if asserted individually can now be aggregated against a common defendant. The Supreme

Court has also effectively rescinded the abstention doctrine, which had called for federal judges to decline to hear cases that rested on questions of state law not yet resolved by the state courts. The Supreme Court has relaxed the rules governing determinations of mootness and, for all intents and purposes, has done away with the political questions doctrine, which had functioned as a limit on judicial activism. The liberalization of rules governing justiciability has given a wider range of litigants access to the courts, has rendered a broader range of issues subject to judicial settlement, and so has greatly increased the reach of the courts in American life. Taken together, these changes help explain the enormous growth over the past three decades in the number of cases handled by the federal judiciary (see figure 5.3).

The federal courts have also come to exercise new powers by expanding the range of remedies and forms of relief they are prepared to employ. Rather than simply ruling that a government agency has violated a plaintiff's rights and ordering that agency to devise remedies, the courts now issue detailed decrees, setting forth the manner in which the agency must thereafter conduct its business. Suits challenging conditions in state prisons, for example, have produced a host of detailed judicial orders that specify living space, recreational programs, and counseling services that must be provided to all prisoners, and that order states to appropriate the necessary funds. Increasingly, judges have also made use of special masters, under the control of the court, to take charge of the day-to-day operations of such institutional defendants as the Boston school system and the Alabama state prison system. The federal judiciary thus can now provide litigants with remedies that historically had been

FIGURE 5.3
THE GROWTH OF FEDERAL JUDICIAL ACTIVITY

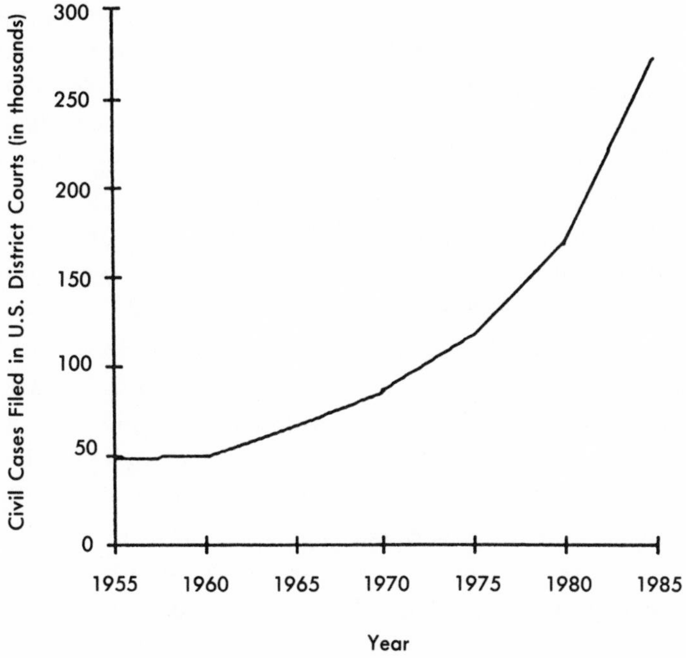

Year

SOURCE: *Statistical Abstracts of the United States* (Washington, D.C.: U.S. Government Printing Office, 1971, 1976, 1987), 152, 168, 169.

available only through the executive and legislative branches.[16]

In the 1960s and 1970s, the most important beneficiaries of these new judicial powers were liberal forces that made litigation a major weapon in their arsenal. Civil rights groups, through federal court suits, launched successful assaults on Southern school systems, state and local governments, and legislative districting schemes; these groups

151

could not possibly have altered such institutions in the electoral arena. Environmental groups used the courts to block the construction of highways, dams, and other public projects that not only threatened to damage the environment but also provided money and other resources to their political rivals. Women's groups were able to overturn state laws restricting abortion as well as statutes discriminating against women in the labor market.

Congress helped liberal interest groups make use of the federal courts for these purposes. A number of regulatory statutes enacted during the 1970s gave public-interest groups the right to bring suits challenging the decisions of executive agencies in environmental cases. Congress also authorized public-interest groups to serve as "private attorneys general" and to finance their activities by collecting legal fees and expenses from their opponents—generally business firms or government agencies—in such suits.

The Supreme Court, for its part, supported Congress in its struggles with the White House. It refused to permit the Nixon administration to block publication of the Pentagon Papers. It ordered the president to turn over the Watergate tapes to the special prosecutor. During the Reagan administration, the Court, in reviewing the constitutionality of the Ethics in Government Act, upheld the designation of special prosecutors as instruments for investigating misconduct in the executive branch.

In the 1970s and 1980s, conservatives reacted to the alliance between liberals and the courts by attempting to restrict the power of the federal judiciary. For example, when the Republicans gained control of the Senate in 1981, North Carolina senator Jesse Helms introduced legislation seeking to strip the Supreme Court of its jurisdiction over a number of matters of concern to the New Right. That same year, the Reagan administration announced a policy of "nonacquiescence" that would limit the courts' ability to interfere with the administration's effort to purge some 490,000 recipients from the Social Security disability rolls. Under this policy, the Social Security Administration would obey lower federal court orders to reinstate a particular individual who had been dropped from the rolls but would not recognize such an order as precedent in any other case. The administration issued assurances that it would recognize U.S. Supreme Court decisions as precedent—but because it planned to avoid appealing adverse rulings to the Supreme Court, there would be no such precedents.

In these and other instances, liberal Democrats took the lead in defending the power and prerogatives of the courts. The Helms court-stripping legislation was defeated in 1981. In 1984, Congress adopted the Social Security Disability Reform Act, which required the administration to accept lower court rulings as precedent in the federal judicial circuit in which they were made. Under further pressure from congressional hearings, the administration in 1985 was forced to abandon the policy of nonacquiescence entirely.[17]

Both Presidents Nixon and Reagan appointed conservative jurists to the federal bench in an effort to curb the liberals' ability to exercise influence through the federal judiciary. During his six years in office, Nixon appointed four justices, including Chief Justice Warren Burger and Associate Justice William Rehnquist, to the Supreme Court. Liberal Democrats sought to block Nixon's efforts to create a conservative majority on the High Court and succeeded in defeating the confirmation of two other conservative jurists, Clement Haynsworth and G. Harold Carswell. The two remaining justices appointed by Nixon, Harry A. Blackmun and Lewis F. Powell, proved to be moderates who were not intent on reversing the Court's direction.

The Reagan administration attempted to ensure that appointees to all levels of the federal bench—district and circuit courts as well as the Supreme Court—were committed conservatives. The administration made a particular effort to appoint conservative legal scholars to federal appeals courts. These scholars included Robert Bork and Ralph K. Winter of Yale; Antonin Scalia, Richard Posner, and Frank Easterbrook of the University of Chicago; Douglas Ginsburg of Harvard; John Noonan of Berkeley; and J. Harvey Wilkerson of the University of Virginia. Through such appointments, the White House hoped to foster an intellectual revolution on the bench and enhance the impact of conservative principles on American jurisprudence.

In the case of the Supreme Court, Reagan appointed Sandra Day O'Connor, a moderate conservative, and Antonin Scalia, whom he had previously named to the circuit court. After a bitter confirmation battle in the Senate, Reagan also was able to elevate William Rehnquist to Chief Justice. Reagan's efforts to place arch-conservative Judge Robert Bork on the high court, however, encountered fierce resistance. Liberal groups organized fund-raising drives and sponsored television advertising in the largest public campaign of the nation's history to defeat a judicial nominee. The administration's opponents on the Senate Judiciary Committee sought to discredit Bork in nationally televised hearings. Rather than examine the nominee's professional competence and ethics, which previously had been seen as the Senate's proper role, they asked him to defend his writings, questioned his philosophy, and sought to ascertain how he would decide major issues likely to face the court. In the end, they rejected the Bork nomination.

Conservative Judge Douglas Ginsburg, whom Reagan nominated in Bork's place, was compelled to withdraw his name from consideration when reporters revealed that while on the faculty of the Harvard Law School he had been seen smoking marijuana. Reagan then named Judge Anthony Kennedy to fill the Court's vacant position. Prodded by members of the Senate Judiciary Committee, Kennedy was compelled to give assurances at his confirmation hearings that he was not intent on overturning Supreme Court precedents. On the strength of these assurances, Kennedy was unanimously confirmed.

Despite the efforts of Senate Democrats, a conservative majority emerged on the Supreme Court after Justice Kennedy's confirmation. In its 1989 term, the Court opened the way for states to place severe restrictions on access to abortion. The Court also ruled against racial minorities in a number of affirmative action and employment discrimination cases, partially overturning liberal civil rights precedents from the 1960s and 1970s.[18]

The full impact of Republican appointees on the federal courts will not be apparent for a number of years. The Supreme Court's recent decisions, however, may well portend the judiciary's emergence as a conservative bastion in alliance with the presidency. Even before Justice Kennedy's appointment, the Court supported executive authority in cases declaring unconstitutional both the legislative veto and the provision of the Gramm-Rudman Act authorizing a congressional official, the Comptroller-General, to supervise mandated budget cuts.[19] Such a conservative reorientation of the federal courts would be especially significant because of the enormous growth of judicial power that has occurred in recent decades.

POLITICAL CONFLICT AND
INSTITUTIONAL COMBAT

As the Republicans have solidified their grip on the presidency and the Democrats their grip on Congress, political conflict in the United States has increasingly come to involve institutional struggle rather than electoral mobilization. As we have seen, fiscal policy, national security policy, and the judiciary have been both weapons and arenas in this struggle. These are not the only weapons or arenas of contemporary institutional combat. Others have included the federal bureaucracy, the complex of nonprofit organizations and public-interest groups that has developed around federal domestic programs, and the national news media.

The Reagan administration made a determined effort to increase presidential control over cabinet departments and independent government agencies by centralizing authority over the appointment of personnel in the White House and over the issuance of regulations in the Office of Management and Budget (OMB). By centralizing control over appointments, the administration sought to ensure that officials would adhere to the administration's priorities rather than those of the agency for which they worked. By requiring agencies to obtain OMB approval for all regulations they issued, the administration sought to diminish both the influence that congressional oversight committees exercised over administrative agencies and, more generally, the role that the federal bureaucracy plays in American life.[20] Figure 5.4 shows that the number of pages of proposed new federal regulations published annually in the Federal Register did decline during the Reagan era.

These attempts to subject the federal bureaucracy to greater White House control did not go unchallenged.[21] Defenders of existing practices and programs asserted that the administration was trying to stack the bureaucracy with

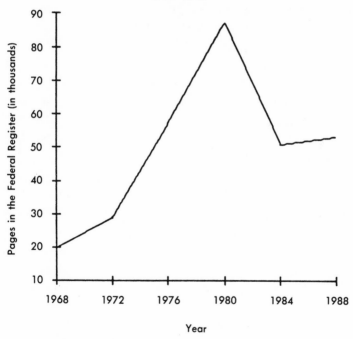

FIGURE 5.4
CHANGE IN FEDERAL REGULATORY ACTIVITY,
1968–1988

SOURCE: Compiled by the authors from *The Federal Register* (Washington, D.C.: U.S. Government Printing Office, 1968–1988).

right-wing ideologues and to interfere with the lawful exercise by Congress of its oversight responsibilities. One way that federal employees responded to what they perceived as a threat to their agencies' integrity was to leak derogatory information about Republican appointees to Congress and the press. Investigations of Housing and Urban Development Secretary Samuel Pierce and Economic Development administrator Carlos Campbell, among others, were fueled by such leaks.

Liberal public-interest groups and nonprofit organizations have also come under attack in recent years. These organizations sustain themselves not only through membership contributions and foundation grants but also through grants from the federal government. Before 1981, recipients of federal funding included such groups as the Reverend Jesse Jackson's Operation PUSH, the Women's Equity Action League, the Conservation Foundation, and numerous organizations that provide social services to the poor. After Reagan's election, presidential appointees to executive agencies sought to "defund the left"—halting the flow of federal funds to finance what the administration regarded as political activities by such groups. For example, the administration cut off funds to legal service agencies that filed class-action suits on behalf of the poor.[22] In addition, the Internal Revenue Service moved to withdraw the tax exemptions of a number of nonprofit advocacy organizations.

The administration's efforts to weaken liberal groups provoked a considerable amount of conflict and controversy. Groups threatened by the conservative offensive resisted by appealing to their allies in Congress, taking their cases to the media, and seeking to mobilize grass-roots support. Social service organizations sought to defend themselves

158

and their constituents by conducting a major voter registration drive among the poor. Reagan's appointees on the board of the Legal Services Corporation responded by initiating an investigation to determine whether the drive constituted a violation of the rights of poor people to decide for themselves whether to register and vote. Ultimately, however, Congress was able to prevent conservative forces in the administration from shutting off the flow of federal funds to advocacy groups.

The national news media—which conservatives regard as liberal bastions—have also been the target of a conservative political offensive in recent years. Libel suits have been key weapons in the conservatives' campaign against the media. (The best known of these was General William Westmoreland's suit against CBS in the early 1980s.) These suits were encouraged and often financed by such conservative organizations as the Capitol Legal Foundation, the American Legal Foundation, and Accuracy in Media, Inc. When accused of chilling critical journalistic investigations of public officials, conservatives forthrightly stated that this was precisely their intent. For example, Reed Irvine, head of Accuracy in Media, asserted that Westmoreland's legal bills were

> footed by contributions from individuals and foundations who believe that CBS deserves to be chilled for the way it treated the general. . . . What is wrong with chilling any propensity of journalists to defame with reckless disregard of the truth?[23]

Despite these libel suits, the national news media continued to be accessible to the Reagan administration's opponents. The press gave extensive coverage to allegations of impropriety against administration officials, especially Attorney General Edwin Meese and White House aides Michael Deaver and Lyn Nofziger. The press also devoted an enormous amount of attention to the charges of mismanagement, malfeasance, and illegal activity in the White House that emerged during the Iran-contra affair. Nevertheless, liberal journalists, such as Anthony Lewis of the *New York Times,* have voiced concern that they and their colleagues have retreated in the face of the contemporary conservative resurgence. The press, they charge, has ignored presidential misstatements of facts, and it has failed to point out the refusal of the Reagan campaign in 1984 and the Bush campaign in 1988 to address real issues.[24]

American politics will continue to center around these and other forms of institutional combat as long as the national electoral arena remains stalemated. The continuation of this political pattern has profound implications for the conduct of government in the United States.

6

Electoral Mobilization, Institutional Combat, and Governmental Power

THE GROWING IMPORTANCE OF institutional forms of political combat has significant consequences for the coherence and vitality of American government. The collapse of political party organizations and the decline of voter turnout have combined to produce a deadlock in the electoral arena that gives the Democrats a stranglehold on Congress and the Republicans a decided edge in contests for the presidency. As each side entrenches itself within its own governmental bastions, American politics is coming to center on the efforts of competing forces to strengthen the institutions they control while undermining those dominated by their opponents. In this way, institutional combat is supplanting electoral competition as the decisive form of political struggle in the United States.

This political pattern undermines the governing capacities of the nation's institutions, diminishing the ability of America's government to manage domestic and foreign affairs, and contributing to the erosion of the nation's international political and economic standing. As long as the American political process is characterized by electoral deadlock and low levels of voter mobilization, this postelectoral system of politics is likely to endure.

INSTITUTIONAL COMBAT AND THE
EROSION OF GOVERNMENTAL POWER

The way that conflict manifests itself in a political system has major implications for the power of government. Where rival militias shoot it out in the streets, as in Lebanon, the government may cease to exercise any authority whatsoever. Conversely, where electoral competition is central, not only can conflicts be settled without bloodshed, but struggles for power can be waged without undermining governmental institutions. Conflicts in the electoral arena over who will govern need not disrupt the government's ability to govern.

The shift from an electorally to an institutionally centered politics in the United States means that efforts by opposing forces to attack and undermine governmental institutions have become major features of political combat. To a growing extent, American politics is taking a form that indeed does impede the government's capacity to govern.[1]

It is true that in the early 1980s Ronald Reagan did impart a sense of direction to American government. The 1980 Republican landslide gave the GOP control of the White House, the Senate, and of enough congressional seats to forge a working majority with conservative Democrats in the House. In 1981 and early 1982, the Reagan administration was able to implement a series of major changes in taxation, expenditure, defense, and regulatory policy, but after little more than a year the pattern of institutional conflict described in the previous chapter reasserted itself. Institutional combat intensified when the Democrats regained effective control of the House in 1983 and of the Senate in 1986. With a few important exceptions—most notably tax reform and the treaty banning intermediate nuclear forces—the administration had difficulty implementing major changes in national policy after 1983.[2] Drift and incoherence largely characterized American government during the balance of the 1980s.

There are three major ways in which contemporary political patterns exacerbate the historic fragmentation of the American state. First, as the Democrats seek to weaken the presidency and to strengthen the administrative and coercive capabilities of Congress while the Republicans attempt to undermine Congress and increase the autonomy of the White House, a system approaching dual sovereignty has emerged in the United States. Second, contemporary electoral processes do not provide for political closure. The question of who will govern is not resolved in elections. As a result, the "winners" have difficulty forming a government, and public officials are compelled to pay as much heed to the impact of policies on domestic struggles as to their implications for collective national purposes. Finally, as bureaucratic agencies have become battlegrounds in, and weapons of, political combat, their ability to effectively implement public policies has been seriously eroded.

163

Dual Sovereignty

Conflict between the political forces controlling Congress and those controlling the presidency is built into the American system of government. Today, however, the separation of powers mandated by the constitution is becoming what amounts to a system of dual sovereignty. In a separation of powers system, the power to govern is shared by disparate institutions. If government is to function, each branch must secure a measure of cooperation from the others. For example, the framers of the constitution provided roles for both the president and Congress in the enactment of legislation. However, the growing prominence of institutional combat in America means that such cooperation often cannot be secured.

A noteworthy example of the extent to which institutional combat has disrupted the system of shared powers is the difficulty President Bush encountered in forming an administration during his first year in office. During the Reagan years, congressional Democrats had effectively used the weaponry of RIP to attack the administration. In its early weeks, the Bush administration found itself similarly threatened by the flood of allegations and revelations that emerged in the course of the Senate's confirmation hearings on the nomination of John Tower to the position of secretary of defense. Ultimately, Democrats were able to defeat Tower, marking the first time in American history that the Senate refused to confirm a cabinet appointment made by a newly elected president.

The Bush administration subsequently adhered to extraordinarily complex procedures to check the backgrounds of appointees, in an effort to protect itself from further attack either in the confirmation process or in the course of later policy conflicts. As a result, during much of Bush's first year in office, hundreds of top-level, policy-making positions remained unfilled, greatly impeding the president's ability to govern.[3]

The increasing prevalence of institutional combat, by disrupting the traditional system of shared powers, has encouraged the major branches of government to develop various formal and informal means of governing autonomously. Thus, the Republicans have undertaken to strengthen the presidency and to enhance its ability to pursue both foreign and domestic objectives independently of Congress. As we have seen, the Reagan administration sought to place control of major foreign and defense policies in the hands of the president's National Security Council. Moreover, it sought to circumvent Congress and rely on the Treasury Department and the Federal Reserve to manage the nation's economy. In a similar vein, through Executive Order 12291, which centralized control over federal regulations in the OMB, President Reagan sought to disrupt ties between Congress and administrative agencies, a disruption that would greatly enhance the legislative powers of the presidency.

The Democrats, for their part, have sought to strengthen Congress and to provide it with the capacity to develop and implement policies independently of the White House. Congress has greatly increased its autonomous control over policy formulation by establishing or bolstering such congressional agencies as the Congressional Budget Office (CBO) and the General Accounting Office (GAO), as well as by expanding the staffs of its committees and subcommittees. As figure 6.1 indicates, over the past two decades the

FIGURE 6.1
THE GROWTH OF HOUSE AND SENATE STAFFS

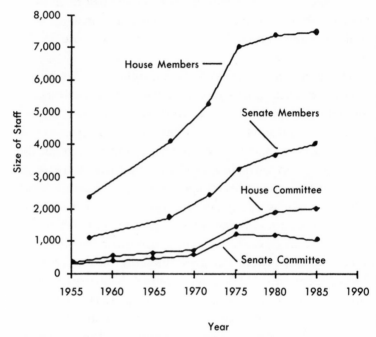

Year

SOURCE: Norman Ornstein et al., *Vital Statistics on Congress* (Washington, D.C.: American Enterprise Institute, 1987), 142, 146.

size of committee staffs has nearly doubled in the Senate and more than tripled in the House. Congress has also enhanced its ability to act autonomously by drafting detailed statutes that reduce the discretion of executive agencies, and by deploying its augmented staff to monitor agency compliance with the priorities of Congress, its committees, and its subcommittees.

Congress and the White House are thus able to pursue independent and even contradictory policies. The example

166

that has most frequently been commented on involves policy toward Central America. At the same time that the administration was seeking to mobilize support in the Central American region for the contra forces in Nicaragua, House Speaker Jim Wright and other members of Congress were conducting their own negotiations with Central American heads of state premised upon American abandonment of the contras. But this is not the only time Congress and the president embarked upon contradictory courses of action. While the Reagan administration was pursuing policies of "constructive engagement" in southern Africa, Congress enacted trade sanctions against the Afrikaner regime. Similarly, while the Reagan administration, concerned with the fate of American military bases, sought to buttress the power of Philippine dictator Ferdinand Marcos, Chairman Stephen Solarz of the House Subcommittee on Asian Affairs was conducting hearings on Marcos's business dealings with the intention of discrediting him. Ultimately, opposition to Marcos in the U.S. Congress and the American media played a central role in the chain of events that led to his ouster.

Despite their various efforts, neither presidents nor Congress have acquired sufficient formal authority to govern autonomously. As a result, they have frequently sought to work through other institutions, including nongovernmental entities. The problems confronting presidents and the Congress are akin to those faced by rulers in early modern Europe. Seeking glory abroad and grandeur at home, but not commanding the apparatus of a modern state, those rulers were compelled to draw on the resources of nongovernmental institutions. Contemporary America possesses such a state apparatus, but neither the White House nor

Congress acting on its own is able to control it fully. The institutional expedients executive and legislative officials have adopted to cope with this problem bear striking resemblances to those devised by Renaissance princes.

Lacking adequate revenue systems, monarchs in the sixteenth and seventeenth centuries made use of tax farmers and bankers for funds.[4] This, in effect, is what the Reagan and Bush administrations have done over the past decade. The United States, of course, created an enormously productive revenue system in the 1940s based upon the progressive income tax. This system permitted politicians to win the support of a host of disparate interests by regularly enacting new spending programs. The Reagan administration managed, through the rate reductions and indexing provisions of the 1981 tax act, to disrupt this regime of interest-group liberalism by reducing the flow of tax receipts upon which it depended. Unable to secure commensurate reductions in domestic spending, however, and committed to an enormously costly military buildup, the administration was compelled to tap new revenue sources. It did so by devising twentieth-century equivalents to the fiscal techniques of Renaissance monarchs, techniques that have endured during the Bush years.

To make up the difference between tax receipts and governmental expenditures, the Reagan and Bush administrations were compelled to borrow $2 trillion through banks and other financial institutions. Approximately one-third of this sum has been supplied by foreign creditors, principally the Japanese. As noted previously, the Reagan and Bush administrations have fought to keep American markets open to Japanese products. Japanese financial institutions, in turn, have used profits earned in the American market (by such firms as Toyota and Sony) to purchase U.S. Treasury securities. The financial relationship between America and Japan was codified in the May 1984 report of the Japan–United States Yen-Dollar Committee.[5] Through this extraordinary relationship, the Japanese supply the U.S. Treasury with monies they collect from American consumers, while of course retaining a healthy share for themselves. This is a system of tax farming in all but name.

The White House has also resorted to fifteenth- and sixteenth-century practices in the realm of foreign and military policy. To bolster their military strength, Renaissance princes depended upon *condottieri,* mercenaries, and privateers.[6] Although the United States possesses an enormous military and intelligence apparatus, since the Vietnam War presidents have had to contend with congressional restrictions on its use. To circumvent limits on its freedom of action in such areas as Central America and Iran, the Reagan administration raised funds from foreign potentates and worked through private firms and free-lance operators like Richard Secord and Albert Hakim to hire mercenaries, organize military operations, and conduct diplomatic negotiations. As in early modern Europe, the conduct of public affairs was placed in private hands.

In modern Europe's formative period, rulers employed private parties not only to make war abroad but also to enforce the law at home. Lacking an extensive administrative apparatus, they relied upon such practices as bounty hunting and rewarding complainants and witnesses in order to assist the identification, apprehension, and prosecution of lawbreakers. For similar reasons, bounty hunting was common on the American frontier through the nineteenth century. Lately, the Congress, lacking full control over an administrative apparatus, has revived these techniques. Regarding environmental regulation, Congress has sought to involve private parties in law enforcement by authorizing citizens to bring suit against alledged polluters.[7] An incentive for such "private attorneys general" has been provided by requirements that convicted polluters pay attorneys' fees that generally far exceed costs to those who brought the suit.

This reversion to tax farming, privateering, and bounty hunting carries with it serious administrative costs. Modern states abandoned these practices precisely because they were inefficient, prone to abuse, and ultimately incompatible with popular sovereignty. Tax farming imposed heavy burdens on citizens while yielding inadequate revenues to the state. Over the past decade, the profits collected from American consumers by foreign manufacturers have greatly exceeded the funds provided by foreign financial institutions to the U.S. Treasury—to say nothing of the interest that the Treasury has obligated itself to pay to foreigners in order to secure these funds. Moreover, this method of raising revenue gives creditors inordinate leverage over the state. As John Brewer says of tax farming in seventeenth-century England, "in surrendering the task of tax gathering to some of its major creditors, the government ran the risk of financial subordination to . . . [a] consortium controlling the two major sources of state income, namely loans and taxes."[8] The United States faces precisely this problem with regard to Japan, which is why the Reagan and Bush administrations have not been in a position to insist that it open its markets to American firms or purchase military aircraft directly from U.S. manufacturers.

States abandoned the use of mercenaries and privateers

because, lacking loyalty to the nation they ostensibly served, they typically placed their own interests first. America relearned this lesson in its dealings with arms merchants and private military contractors in the Iran-contra affair. And just as bounty hunters were indifferent to larger public concerns such as the rights of the accused, private litigants cannot be expected to consider the ramifications for other public goals and policies of the suits they choose to bring— for example, the economic burden of alternative methods of pollution control. Thus administrative expedients that were already inadequate in the early modern era are even less well suited to the governance of a twentieth-century state.

No Winners, No Losers

The political developments of the past twenty years also produce weak and divided governments. Under present circumstances, electoral competition does not create winners with the power to make and implement policies, nor does it substantially reduce the losers' opportunities to exercise influence. This absence of political closure exacerbates the historical fragmentation of the American state and leads to a policy-making process that is not well suited to the achievement of collective national purposes. Increasingly, four characteristics have come to dominate the formulation and implementation of public policy in the United States: support-shopping, burden-shifting, weapon-forging, and political paralysis. These features are by no means new to the American policy-making process, but they have become intensified at the very time that the United States faces

171

competitive pressures from states whose policy-making processes are more coherent.

In the case of support-shopping, the persistence of divided control of government and the intensification of institutional conflict means that presidential proposals are as likely to be greeted with suspicion as enthusiasm on Capitol Hill. Presidents are able to strike deals with the leadership of Congress on some issues, but they often must shop for support on an issue-by-issue, member-by-member basis. As a result, all programs tend to acquire a distributive component: Support is purchased by providing members of Congress with specific benefits for the interests or constituencies they represent, raising the costs of government programs and diffusing their impact.

This is true even of Reagan's notable legislative successes—the 1981 tax cut, the 1981 and 1982 budget cuts, and the 1986 tax reform act.[9] To assemble a majority for its tax cut proposal in 1981, for example, the Reagan administration was compelled to bid for the support of members of Congress by offering major exemptions and deductions to a host of special interests, including manufacturers, small business, and the oil industry. Reagan's budget director, David Stockman, estimates that this almost doubled the cost to the Treasury of the administration's tax cut proposal; over a period of ten years, adding $870 billion to the $983 billion cut that the administration proposed.[10] This contributed greatly to subsequent budget deficits.

The necessity of building majorities on a piecemeal basis also enables members of Congress to demand that, in exchange for their support, the interests for which they speak be relieved of the costs and burdens associated with new programs. This allows powerful interests to shift these bur-

172

dens to others—often to the public treasury. For example, early in the Bush administration, the Treasury Department's initial plan for resolving the crisis in the savings and loan (S&L) industry involved imposing a fee on S&L deposits. This idea was adamantly rejected by the industry and met overwhelming resistance on Capitol Hill, where thrift institutions enjoy a good deal of influence. The administration was compelled to disown the Treasury plan, and it proposed instead a plan in which general tax revenues would finance the bulk of the cost of the $150 billion bailout. In this way, a powerful interest was able to shift the burden of a major federal initiative designed for the industry's own benefit from itself to the general public. To mask the impact that the bail-out would have on the nation's budget deficit, the administration proposed to finance much of it through "off-budget" procedures—a ploy that would eventually add billions of dollars to the cost of the program.

The absence of political closure has a third implication for the formation of public policy. Because conflicts are not resolved in the electoral arena and continue unabated within the governmental process, public officials must focus on the implications of programs and policies for institutional struggles as a condition for exercising power. Under these circumstances, contending forces undertake to forge weapons of institutional combat as much as to serve collective national purposes when fashioning public policies.

This tendency is exacerbated by the diminution of accountability in contemporary American politics. When there are no clearcut winners and losers, responsibility for the success or failure of policies to address national problems is diffused, and public officials are better able to avoid being held accountable for the consequences of their decisions.[11] This lessened accountability diminishes what might otherwise be a major constraint upon politicians' willingness to give priority to the pursuit of institutional and political advantage when fashioning policies.

The Reagan and Bush administrations' tolerance of enormous budget deficits and their program of deregulation provide examples of this phenomenon. As was noted previously, a major reason why Republican administrations have been prepared to accept the economic risks of unprecedented deficits is the constraint these deficits impose on congressional power. Similarly, the Republicans have pressed for deregulation in part because the congeries of interests that surround many regulatory policies are important Democratic bastions. In this effort, the administration often overlooked potential costs and risks. For instance, relaxation of regulatory restraints on financial institutions permitted many S&Ls to shift from their traditional role as home mortgage lenders into potentially more lucrative but dangerously speculative areas. Even as many S&Ls began to suffer heavy losses, the administration's commitment to deregulation did not wane.

A concern for institutional and political advantage can also color the way officials respond to the initiatives of their opponents. For example, congressional Democrats regularly vote for lower levels of military spending than the White House proposes, not because they are less committed to the nation's defense, but because they have come to identify the defense establishment as an important institutional bastion of the Republicans.

Finally, contemporary electoral processes can lead to political paralysis because they reinforce governmental fragmentation and division. In a number of important areas, institutional divisions have impeded the federal government from responding to situations that both Democrats and Republicans regard as important national problems. Bipartisan commissions, whose members are composed of both presidential and congressional appointees, are one device to which policy makers have resorted on a number of recent occasions to deal with problems that the regular institutions of government found themselves unable to handle. Such commissions were created to resolve conflicts over the impending collapse of the Social Security system, the closing of military bases, the basing of MX missiles, the crisis in Central America, and the budget deficit.[12] The first two of these commissions were successful, but the remaining three were unable to overcome the deep divisions between Congress and the White House.

The Destruction of Administrative Capacity

Contemporary patterns of institutional combat exacerbate the administrative incoherence of the American state. Over the past two decades, Congress and the political forces with which it is allied have sought to acquire administrative capacities independent of the White House. Congress has restricted the discretion of presidentially appointed administrative officials, increased committee and subcommittee involvement in agency decision making, opened agencies to direct interest-group participation in administrative rule making, and expanded opportunities for judicial intervention in administration. These efforts promote fragmentation in the executive branch and can disrupt administrative processes. Attempts by the White House to reassert its authority

175

over the executive branch have often done more to inten-
sify than to remedy these problems.

One way in which Congress and its allies have sought to
gain control over administrative processes is by drafting
legislation that specifies in great detail the standards governing administrative conduct. The most familiar examples
are the environmental statutes enacted during the 1970s,
which set strict standards for air and water quality and the
means through which they are to be met. The statutes have
often precluded administrators from taking account of
changes in technology, cost considerations, economic impact, and other public ends in supervising industry compliance with the legislation.[13]

Congress has also undertaken to subject administrative
agencies to control by its committees and subcommittees.[14]
Over the past twenty-five years, the number of subcommittees in the House of Representatives has increased by more
than 25 percent to 130, and the size of committee and
subcommittee staffs has more than tripled. These increases
have enabled Congress to scrutinize more closely than ever
before the activities of administrative agencies, both
through direct supervision by congressional staff and
through frequent oversight hearings. In addition, by including legislative veto provisions in statutes and issuing detailed committee reports that the courts recognize as evidence of legislative intent, Congress gives its committees
control over agency decisions.

Congress's ability to prevent the Reagan administration
from imposing its own priorities on the Legal Services Corporation (LSC) provides some of the most striking examples
of this phenomenon.[15] During the 1960s and 1970s, Legal
Services attorneys won numerous class-action suits expand-

ing the rights of welfare recipients, tenants in public housing projects, and the clients of other public programs serving the poor. During its first year in office, the Reagan administration sought to abolish the corporation, but this move was blocked by Congress. The administration was able, however, to appoint a majority of the corporation's directors, and they urged that agency attorneys focus their efforts exclusively on routine domestic relations and personal credit problems rather than class-action suits and political advocacy.

Congressional subcommittees with jurisdiction over the agency were able to completely frustrate the administration's efforts. When the new board sought to introduce accounting and reporting requirements that would enable it to monitor the activities of staff attorneys, Congress responded to appeals from agency staffers and killed the requirements. This effectively prevented the board from ascertaining how agency funds were spent and how employees spent their time. Congressional subcommittees also blocked the board's efforts to eliminate funding for programs it sought to abolish. In addition, the chairman of the Senate subcommittee with jurisdiction over the agency's appropriations prevented the board from implementing a regulation that would have prohibited legal service lawyers from engaging in lobbying and other political activities. In the case of the LSC, as in many others, congressional committees and subcommittees all but took charge of running an agency. Because there are more than 250 of these congressional units, their increasing role in administration is leading toward the emergence of a plural executive in the United States.

During the past two decades, the coherence of the American state has also been undermined by the growing involvement of interest groups in administrative decision making. Having no commitment to executive prerogatives, Congress increasingly has authorized interest groups to participate directly in administrative rule making. Groups that enjoy access to Congress can, in effect, write their own priorities into law.

For example, the 1972 act establishing the Consumer Product Safety Commission (CPSC) established a process through which consumer groups could petition the agency to regulate new products and even develop specific rules for the agency to adopt. In 1981, pro-business forces were able to defeat consumer forces in Congress, amending the act so as to give business the same sort of influence over CPSC rule making that consumer groups had formerly enjoyed. The agency, for instance, was now required to invite product manufacturers to propose voluntary safety standards and to give these preference over its own mandatory rules.[16]

Finally, Congress has greatly increased the role of the courts in administrative processes. The courts' increased role provides another channel for interest groups to exert influence over executive agencies, and it often hinders agencies from carrying out any administrative task opposed by any group or individual with the resources to hire a lawyer. For example, the 1970 statute that established the EPA provided interest groups with opportunities to appeal virtually every agency decision in the courts. This has compelled the EPA to adopt such cumbersome decision-making procedures that it has difficulty accomplishing anything at all.[17]

The White House's response to efforts by Congress and

its allies to assert control over administrative agencies has often sparked conflicts that further undermine the capacity and coherence of the executive branch. During the Nixon years, for example, the administration imposed personnel ceilings on agencies it deemed to be too closely tied to Congress, resulting in hampered agency performance. Congress responded by adopting legislation setting strict personnel floors for the agencies involved. Frozen by statute, these floors reduced managerial flexibility and agency efficiency.[18] In the Reagan and Bush years, conflicts between the White House and Congress have disrupted the functioning of a number of departments and agencies, including the Justice Department, the EPA, the Civil Rights Commission, and the Economic Development Administration.

Governmental Power and American Competitiveness

The erosion of the power and coherence of American government contributes to the difficulties the nation is experiencing in the international realm. In particular, dual sovereignty, the absence of clear-cut winners and losers, and the disruption of administrative capabilities together produce public policies that undermine America's economic competitiveness.

Most important, struggles between the White House and Congress have led to fiscal policies that are likely to damage the American economy. The Reagan administration's insistence on simultaneously cutting taxes and increasing military spending, coupled with Congress's refusal to reduce spending on entitlement programs, generated enormous budget deficits, which the White House has been willing to tolerate as a way of restraining Congress.

The monies borrowed to finance these deficits will have to be repaid from the nation's future income. Had the borrowed funds been invested in ways that increased the productivity of the American economy rather than mainly consumed in defense and entitlement spending, this would pose few problems: Economic growth would then supply the income to repay the debt. Because deficits have been used to finance current consumption, however, their repayment will reduce future national income and economic growth. By drawing down the nation's pool of savings, deficits also reduce the availability of domestic funds for investment in the productive resources and new technologies that would enhance the future international competitiveness of the American economy.[19]

Another dimension of the deficit problem is its implication for foreign penetration of American markets. During the early years of the Reagan administration, the deficit, combined with the restrictive monetary policies pursued by the Federal Reserve, drove up real interest rates in the United States and the value of the American dollar. This enabled foreign firms to penetrate the American market. Ultimately, the growing trade deficit—and the measures to cope with it taken in 1985 and 1986 by the United States and its major trading partners—caused the value of the dollar to fall. By this time, however, many American firms had been driven out of business, foreign manufacturers had established production facilities and distribution networks in the United States, and American consumers had developed a taste for foreign goods.

Finally, the heavy borrowing upon which the Reagan and Bush administrations have relied to finance government expenditures provides foreigners with an ever-growing claim on the national income of the United States. The repayment of principal and interest on the hundreds of billions of dollars in U.S. Treasury securities purchased by foreign investors will drain enormous sums of money from the American economy for decades to come. A tempting response to this problem is to repudiate some of this debt by devaluing the U.S. currency and repaying foreigners with dollars worth less than those they initially lent. Indeed, this is precisely what was accomplished when the value of the dollar—and hence of foreign holdings of U.S. debt— was cut in half in 1985–1986. However, what may appear to be the easy way out comes at a price. Devaluation of the dollar contributes to inflation and enables foreigners to purchase American factories, farms, and commercial real estate at bargain-basement prices. This helps to explain why foreign ownership of U.S. assets has increased markedly since the mid-1980s (see figure 6.2). The profits earned on these assets provide overseas nationals with still another claim on future U.S. income. Thus, there is no way to escape the adverse impact that continuing budget deficits impose on America's international economic position and future standard of living.[20]

Another way in which the growing incoherence of American government undermines the nation's competitiveness is through its effects on U.S. trade policy. Because policy-makers find it difficult to impose costs on entrenched interests, American trade policy is often driven more by political than strategic calculation. In contrast to Japanese practice in the manufacturing sector, the United States protects domes-

FIGURE 6.2
FOREIGN OWNERSHIP OF U.S. ASSETS, 1970–1986

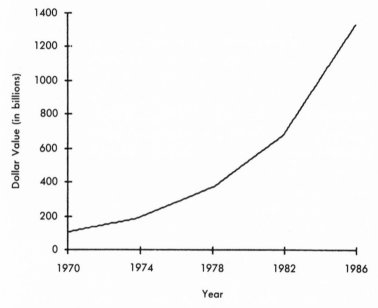

SOURCE: *The Economic Report of the President* (Washington, D.C.: U.S. Government Printing Office, 1983, 1988), 281, 369.

tic industries (such as the steel, textile, and footwear industries) that possess significant political leverage without requiring them to reorganize in ways that would enhance their competitiveness.

At the same time, efforts to help American firms secure access to foreign markets are often undermined by contemporary political patterns. The White House's dependence on Japan to finance the budget deficit has led both the Reagan and Bush administrations to resist efforts to restrict Japanese access to American markets and to be less than vigorous in their efforts to open Japanese markets to American firms. Thus, the administration has not insisted that Japan open its markets in telecommunications, construction, financial services, and agricultural products—markets in which American firms would be competitive.

The incapacity of American administrative institutions also diminishes the nation's economic competitiveness. Administrative incoherence has, for example, impeded the development of domestic energy sources, such as nuclear power, and contributed to America's growing dependence on foreign energy supplies. The process through which the Nuclear Regulatory Commission (NRC) licenses new power plants is subject to intervention at multiple stages by interest groups, members of Congress, and state and local officials. As a result, it now takes five years to obtain an operating license for a nuclear plant, a delay that has contributed to a sevenfold increase over the past twenty years in the capital costs of new nuclear plants. The less cumbersome regulatory processes employed in Western Europe and Japan produce nuclear power plants every bit as safe as American plants much more rapidly and far less expensively. While the U.S. economy is increasingly burdened by the costs and risks of imported energy, America's major trading partners are shedding these burdens.[21]

ELECTORAL MOBILIZATION AND
GOVERNMENTAL POWER

The relationship between political patterns and governmental effectiveness is a complex one. Practices that severely undermine governmental capacities in some settings may not in others—witness the ability of Japan to thrive despite widespread political corruption. But, in the United States and elsewhere, political patterns have at times emerged that have seriously inhibited governments from pursuing collective purposes. For example, in Israel during the late 1980s, electoral stalemate between the Labor and Likud parties paralyzed the government. This stalemate prevented the government from responding effectively to uprisings in the occupied territories and to diplomatic initiatives by the Palestine Liberation Organization, thereby threatening the relationship with the United States, which is a necessary condition for Israel's very survival.

Similar examples can be found in American history. In the United States during the early 1930s, prevailing political patterns led the government to pursue policies that exacerbated rather than ameliorated the Depression. A particularly notable example is the Smoot-Hawley tariff of 1930. The logrolling practices that at the time characterized the formulation of trade policy in the U.S. Congress led to the adoption of the highest tariffs in American history. This precipitated foreign retaliation, a virtual collapse of international trade, and helped turn what could have been an ordinary cyclical downturn into the most severe economic crisis of the modern era. Even more striking than the events of the early 1930s were those preceding the Civil War. Political paralysis during the Buchanan administration prevented the government from responding to its own dismemberment as southern states seceded from the Union.

Historically, efforts to overcome political patterns that undermine governmental effectiveness have taken one of two forms in the United States: political demobilization or mobilization. Demobilization involves attempts to free government from "political interference" by insulating decision-making processes, restricting political participation, or both. Mobilization consists of efforts by one or another contender for power to overcome political stalemate and governmental paralysis by bringing new voters into the electorate and winning over some of the opposition's supporters. In this way, a party can overwhelm its opponents in the electoral arena and take full control of the institutions of government. Such a strategy also provides a party with a mass base of support that can enable it to confront and prevail over entrenched social and economic interests.

Demobilization and insulation were the paths followed by institutional reformers in the United States during the Progressive era. The Progressives, who spoke for a predominately middle-class constituency, sought to cope with the problems of turn-of-the-century America by strengthening the institutions of national, state, and local government. Progressives undertook to strengthen executive institutions by promoting civil service reform, creating regulatory commissions staffed by experts, and transferring fiscal and administrative responsibilities from elected to appointed officials.[22] In addition, asserting that the intrusion of partisan considerations undermined governmental efficiency, the Progressives attacked state and local party organizations. They sponsored legislative investigations of ties between party leaders and businessmen and the criminal prosecution of politicians they deemed to be corrupt.[23] The Progressives also supported the enactment of personal registration requirements for voting that served to reduce turnout among the poorly educated, immigrant, nonwhite, and working-class voters who had provided party organizations with their mass base.[24] Partly as a result of these measures, voter participation rates in the United States fell by nearly thirty percentage points during the first quarter of the twentieth century, a decline from which they never fully recovered.[25]

In the short run, the Progressive strategy of administrative reform did help to enhance governmental capacities in the United States. Government agencies penetrated by parties and rife with patronage are not well suited to performing the functions of a modern state. However, politicians are not in a position to prevail over entrenched social and economic forces when they lack the support of an extensive and well-organized mass constituency. In the long run, the Progressive strategy of insulation and demobilization undermined the strength of American government relative to powerful interests in civil society and helped to produce the low rates of voter turnout that contribute to political stalemate in the United States today.

The second strategy—political mobilization—was used most effectively in the United States by the administrations of Abraham Lincoln and Franklin D. Roosevelt. To fight the Civil War and break the power of Southern slaveholders, the Lincoln administration vastly expanded the scope of the American national state. It raised an enormous army and created a national system of taxation, a national currency, and a national debt. The extensive organizing and extraordinary popular mobilization that brought the Republicans to power in 1860 enabled them to raise more than two million troops, to sell more than $2 billion in bonds to finance the military effort, and to rally popular support for the war. The higher levels of party organization and political mobilization in the North than in the South, as much as the superiority of Northern industry, help explain the triumph of the Union cause in the Civil War.[26]

The Roosevelt administration permanently transformed the American institutional landscape, creating the modern welfare and regulatory state.[27] The support which the administration mobilized through party organizations and labor unions helped it contend with opposition to its programs both inside and outside the institutions of government. A marked increase in electoral turnout, a realignment of some existing blocs of voters, and a revitalized Democratic party apparatus provided Roosevelt with the enormous majorities in the Electoral College and Congress that allowed him to secure the enactment of his programs.[28] Worker mobilization through unions and strikes forced businessmen to accept the new pattern of industrial relations the administration was seeking to establish.[29]

Demobilization Versus Mobilization in Contemporary Politics

The dangers facing the United States in the 1990s are not as immediate as those that the nation confronted on the eve of the Civil War or in the aftermath of the 1929 stock market crash. Nevertheless, America's political processes impede governmental responses adequate to the challenges that the nation faces. This impediment is contributing to the difficulties now confronting America in the international economic arena.

Of the political expedients adopted and the solutions proposed in recent years for the nation's problems, the majority follow the first of the aforementioned paths—that of political insulation and demobilization. Thus, the often-proposed constitutional amendment requiring a balanced budget would deprive elected officials of discretion over fiscal policy. The bipartisan commissions—increasingly used to overcome governmental stalemate—represent an attempt to insulate government decisions from political pressure. And there are clear demobilizing implications in recent calls for the Democratic party to distance itself from racial minorities so as to become more competitive in presidential elections.[30]

Whatever advantages might be derived from such expedients in the short run, they raise issues of democratic legitimacy and, as the experience of Progressivism suggests, in the long run they are likely to weaken government. The founders of the American republic recognized that a strong national government could not be built in the United States on a narrow popular base. As James Wilson observed at the Constitutional Convention of 1787, "raising the federal pyramid to a considerable altitude" required giving it "as broad a base as possible."[31]

It is precisely the narrow base of the "federal pyramid" that underlies governmental disarray in the United States today. As we have suggested in this book, the decay of American electoral democracy—particularly the destruction of party organizations and erosion of voter turnout—has contributed to electoral deadlock and the consequent emergence of alternative forms of political struggle. This pattern of politics undermines governmental institutions and further discourages voter participation. In its origins, character, and consequences, America's postelectoral political order is linked to low levels of popular participation in politics.

America's current political and governmental disarray is

unlikely to be overcome as long as the electoral deadlock of the past quarter century persists. Breaking this deadlock would probably require one or the other party to engage in political mobilization. The probability that this path will be taken, however, is not great.

Were one of the parties to mobilize and forge organizational links to new voters, it might put itself in a position to gain control of all the major institutions of government. At the same time, mobilization could provide the party with a political base enabling it to prevail over entrenched interests and powerful social forces for the sake of achieving collective national purposes. Under such circumstances, the most debilitating features of the contemporary American policy-making process might be contained.

For the Democrats, a strategy of mobilization presumably would involve a serious effort to bring into the electorate the tens of millions of working-class and poor Americans who presently stand entirely outside the political process. Figure 6.3 illustrates the large gap between the voting participation rates of Americans in upper-middle-, lower-middle-, and working-class occupations. Bringing citizens who currently do not vote into the Democratic party would probably require an organizational and programmatic focus on economic issues that unite poor, working-, and lower-middle-class voters rather than the racial and cultural issues that divide them.

Though it is generally assumed that only the Democrats could benefit from any substantial expansion of the electorate, it is important to note that mobilization is a strategy that could be employed by the Republicans as well.[32] Indeed, in the late 1970s and early 1980s it was the GOP, through its alliance with conservative evangelicals, that made the more

FIGURE 6.3
OCCUPATIONAL STRATA AND VOTING TURNOUT,
1984*

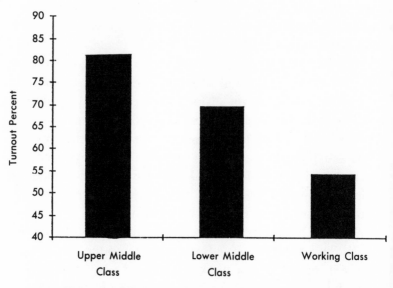

SOURCE: University of Michigan Institute for Social Research. Data were made available through the Inter-University Consortium for Political and Social Research.
*Turnout figures based on survey data overstate actual participation rates.

concerted effort to bring new voters into the electorate. The extent of Republican organizational efforts was limited, however, and thus so was the party's ability to construct a base of support for conservatism large enough to pose a challenge to Democratic congressional hegemony.

By contrast, Europe's great conservative mobilizers of the nineteenth century, Otto von Bismarck and Benjamin Disraeli, brought millions of new working-class voters into the electorate and constructed extensive party organizations to link them securely to the conservative cause. By sponsoring factory and social legislation, moreover, they appealed to these voters on the basis of their long-term economic concerns, not simply their religious and nationalistic passions. Their counterpart in the United States, Abraham Lincoln, proceeded along similar lines. Nineteenth-century Republican electoral mobilization entailed the construction of party organizations throughout the North and relied on economic appeals as much as on the issues of slavery and union. The most important Republican slogan in 1860, after all, was "Vote yourself a farm, vote yourself a tariff." As these examples suggest, its position as the more conservative of the two major parties does not preclude the contemporary GOP from organizing a broad popular base for itself.

It is not likely, however, that either Democrats or Republicans will be willing to embark on the path of full-scale political mobilization. The electoral histories of both America and Europe demonstrate that strong party organizations are necessary to achieve high levels of electoral participation, particularly at the bottom half of the social scale. Massive organizational efforts would be required to reach the 50 percent of the potential electorate not drawn to the polls by present-day electoral techniques and appeals. These efforts would be difficult in the face of legal and institutional impediments—ranging from voter registration laws to communications technologies—that currently strengthen individual politicians relative to parties. The enactment of legislation such as the National Voter Registration Act of 1989 might be a halting step in the direction of fuller electoral participation. But by leaving the burden of registration on the individual voter, such legislation hardly seems likely to reach the millions of poor and poorly educated individuals who constitute the hard core of the nonvoting population.

The most important barriers to full-scale voter mobilization in the United States, however, are not legal or technological; they are political. The politicians who have risen to the top in contemporary America learned their skills and succeeded in a low-mobilization environment. And the weapons of institutional combat that have become central in American politics contribute to maintaining such an environment. When they rely mainly on these weapons to compete with one another, politicians provide voters with little opportunity or reason to participate in politics.

For example, the principal focus of partisan conflict during the first year of the Bush administration was a sequence of revelations and investigations through which the Democrats and Republicans attempted to discredit one another. The Democrats' attack on the drinking habits and sexual conduct of Bush defense secretary designee John Tower was followed by a Republican attack on the personal finances of House Speaker Jim Wright and Democratic Whip Tony Coelho, which was followed by Democratic attacks upon the ethics of Republican House Whip Newt Gingrich and Republican attacks on the personal conduct of Democratic Representative Barney Frank. Gingrich had bolstered his candidacy for the second-highest position in the House Republican leadership by initiating the charges against Wright, and Frank had enhanced his prominence among House Democrats with his sharp criticisms of former attorney general Ed Meese's financial dealings. Thus the RIP process is now being used both to make and unmake political careers. Unlike the electoral processes through which politicians formerly won or lost power, contemporary weapons of institutional combat leave little room for popular participation. Indeed, when they use weapons of institutional combat to discredit one another, political leaders give voters new reasons to refrain from participating.

Conversely, politicians competing for the support of a highly mobilized electorate would have to deal with questions of concern to tens of millions of voters and would not find it possible to focus on the issues of personal impropriety that loom so large in American politics today. Nor would they find themselves so vulnerable to such charges. In 1944, for example, when Republicans charged that Franklin Roosevelt had used government property for his personal benefit by sending a U.S. Navy destroyer to retrieve a pet he had left behind on the Aleutian Islands, the president ridiculed them for attacking "my little dog, Fala."[33] FDR's links to a mass constituency were too strong to be threatened by the GOP charges, and therefore he was in a position to dismiss them with a derisive quip. Lacking such support, elected officials today are much more vulnerable to allegations of personal impropriety.

In contrast to the immediate gains that can be realized today by using revelations and investigations to drive opponents from office, the path of mobilization would entail major risks for both parties. For the Republicans, expansion of the electorate could threaten the advantage they currently enjoy in the arena of presidential elections. As for the Democrats, whatever the potential benefits to the party as a whole, an influx of millions of new voters would create serious uncertainties for current officeholders at the local, state, and congressional levels. Moreover, various interests allied with the Democrats—notably upper-middle-class environmentalists, public-interest lawyers, antinuclear activists, and the like—could not be confident of retaining their

193

influence in a more fully mobilized electoral environment. Finally, though it is seldom openly admitted, the truth is that many members of both the liberal and conservative camps are wary of fuller popular participation in American politics. Conservatives fear blacks, and liberals often have disdain for working- and lower-middle-class whites.

As long as these conditions persist, the path of electoral mobilization will not be taken. America's postelectoral political patterns, governmental incapacities, and economic difficulties will endure—and America will continue to pay the price of its undemocratic politics.

Notes

CHAPTER 1

1 Walter Dean Burnham, "The Turnout Problem," in *Elections American Style,* ed. A. James Reichley (Washington, D.C.: Brookings Institution, 1987), 97–133.

2 Burdett Loomis, *The New American Politician* (New York: Basic Books, 1988).

3 Julie Rovner, "Turnover in Congress Hits an All-Time Low," *Congressional Quarterly Weekly Report* (19 Nov. 1988): 3362–63.

4 David Mayhew, "Congressional Elections: The Case of the Vanishing Marginals," *Polity* 6 (1974): 295–317.

5 Jeremy Rabkin, *Judicial Compulsions* (New York: Basic Books, 1989).

6 Martin Shapiro, "The Supreme Court's 'Return' to Economic Regulation," *Studies in American Political Development* 1 (1986): 91–142.

7 William Keller, *The Liberals and J. Edgar Hoover* (Princeton: Princeton University Press, 1989), chap. 5.

8 Martin Shefter, *Political Crisis/Fiscal Crisis* (New York: Basic Books, 1985), chap. 2.

9   David Broder, *The Party's Over* (New York: Harper & Row, 1971); Larry Sabato, *The Rise of Political Consultants* (New York: Basic Books, 1981); Martin Wattenberg, *The Decline of American Political Parties* (Cambridge, Mass.: Harvard University Press, 1986).

10 See especially Walter Dean Burnham, *The Current Crisis in American Politics* (New York: Oxford University Press, 1982).

11 Morris Fiorina, *Congress: Keystone of the Washington Establishment* (New Haven: Yale University Press, 1977).

12 On the Democrats' advantage in congressional districting, see Rhodes Cook, "Parties in High-Stakes Battle for Right to Draw Lines," *Congressional Quarterly Weekly Report* (12 Aug. 1989): 2137–44; and Gary King and Andrew Gelman, "Systemic Consequences of Incumbency Advantage in U.S. House Elections" (unpublished paper, Dept. of Government, Harvard University, 20 Jan. 1989). On the Democrats' advantage in mobilizing campaign activists, see, for example, Linda Fowler and Robert D. McClure, *Political Ambition: Who Decides to Run for Congress* (New Haven, Conn.: Yale University Press, 1989), 210–17.

13 Samuel Kernell, "Campaigning, Governing, and the Contemporary Presidency," in *The New Direction in American Politics,* ed. John Chubb and Paul Peterson (Washington, D.C.: Brookings Institution, 1985), 117–42.

14 Thomas Byrne Edsall, "The Reagan Legacy," in *The Reagan Legacy,* ed. Sidney Blumenthal and Thomas Byrne Edsall (New York: Pantheon, 1988), 3–50; William Schneider, "The Political Legacy of the Reagan Years," in *The Reagan Legacy,* 51–98.

15 Edward G. Carmines and James Stimson, *Issue Evolution: The Racial Transformation of American Politics* (Princeton: Princeton University Press, 1988); see also Robert Weissberg,

"The Democratic Party and the Conflict Over Racial Policy," in *Do Elections Matter?* ed. Benjamin Ginsberg and Alan Stone (Armonk, N.Y.: M.E. Sharpe, 1986), 204–20.

16 Rhodes Cook, "GOP Planning to Woo Blacks to Widen Its Local Base," *Congressional Quarterly Weekly Report* (4 March 1989): 474–77.

17 Frances Fox Piven and Richard A. Cloward, *Why Americans Don't Vote* (New York: Pantheon, 1988).

18 David R. Mayhew, "Does it Make a Difference Whether Party Control of American National Government Is Unified or Divided?" (paper presented at the 1989 annual meeting of the American Political Science Association, Atlanta, Georgia, 31 Aug.–3 Sept. 1989).

19 Alexander Bickel, *The Supreme Court and the Idea of Progress* (New York: Harper & Row, 1970).

20 Mark Silverstein and Benjamin Ginsberg, "The Supreme Court and the New Politics of Judicial Power," *Political Science Quarterly* 102 (Fall 1987): 371–88.

21 Samuel P. Huntington, "The Defense Policy of the Reagan Administration," in *The Reagan Presidency: An Early Assessment,* ed. Fred Greenstein (Baltimore: Johns Hopkins University Press, 1983), 82–87.

22 James MacGregor Burns, *Roosevelt: The Lion and the Fox* (New York: Harcourt, Brace & World, 1956).

23 Neil Sheehan, *A Bright Shining Lie* (New York: Random House, 1988).

24 Daniel C. Hallin, *The Uncensored War* (Berkeley: University of California Press, 1986).

25 Samuel P. Huntington, *American Politics: The Promise of Disharmony* (Cambridge, Mass.: Harvard University Press, 1981), 203–10.

26 Richard Nathan, *The Plot That Failed: Nixon's Administrative Presidency* (New York: John Wiley, 1975).

27 David Stockman, *The Triumph of Politics* (New York: Harper & Row, 1986).

28 Recent events in the Department of Interior follow the same pattern. See Emily Smith and Vicky Cahan, "Interior Is a House Divided: Bickering Between Branches and Charges of Altered Reports," *Business Week* (24 April 1989): 52.

CHAPTER 2

1 On the role of business during the New Deal compare the analysis of Thomas Ferguson, "From Normalcy to New Deal: Industrial Structure, Party Competition, and American Public Policy in the Great Depression," *International Organization* 38 (Winter 1984): 42–94, with Theda Skocpol and John Ikenberry, "The Political Formation of the American Welfare State," *Comparative Social Research* 6 (1983): 87–148.

2 Peter Gourevitch, *Politics in Hard Times* (Ithaca: Cornell University Press, 1986), chap. 3.

3 Theodore J. Lowi, *The End of Liberalism,* 2nd ed. (New York: W. W. Norton, 1979), chap. 3. See also Benjamin I. Page, *Who Gets What From Government* (Berkeley: University of California Press, 1983).

4 Nancy J. Weiss, *Farewell to the Party of Lincoln* (Princeton: Princeton University Press, 1983).

5 Frances Fox Piven and Richard A. Cloward, *Poor People's Movements* (New York: Vintage Books, 1979), chap. 4.

6 To be sure, northern liberals found southern racial practices morally abhorrent, and for this reason they had supported antilynching legislation in Congress in the 1930s. But they were prepared to risk shattering the Democratic coalition with a crusade against segregation only when additional considerations led them in this direction. For an excellent analy-

sis of these issues, see C. Vann Woodward, *The Strange Career of Jim Crow* (New York: Oxford University Press, 1974).

7 Martin Shefter, "Party, Bureaucracy, and Political Change in the United States," in *Political Parties: Development and Decay,* ed. Louis Maisel and Joseph Cooper, Sage Electoral Studies Yearbook 4 (Beverly Hills: Sage Publications, 1978), 243–54.

8 Michael Paul Rogin, *The Intellectuals and McCarthy: The Radical Specter* (Cambridge, Mass.: The M. I. T. Press, 1967), chap. 8.

9 Franz Schurmann, *The Logic of World Power* (New York: Pantheon Books, 1974), 127.

10 Imanuel Wallerstein, "Friends as Foes," *Foreign Policy* 40 (Fall 1980): 119–31.

11 David Vogel, "The Public Interest Movement and the American Reform Tradition," *Political Science Quarterly* 95 (Winter 1980–1981): 607–27.

12 Nelson Polsby, *Consequences of Party Reform* (New York: Oxford University Press, 1983).

13 David Vogel, "The Power of Business in America: A Reappraisal," *British Journal of Political Science* 13 (January 1983): 19–44.

14 On the declining electoral significance of party identification and the growing importance of issues in shaping voter behavior during the 1960s and 1970s, see Norman Nie, Sidney Verba, and John Petrocik, *The Changing American Voter* (Cambridge, Mass.: Harvard University Press, 1979).

15 Walter Dean Burnham, *The Current Crisis in American Politics* (New York: Oxford University Press, 1982), chap. 9.

16 Austin Ranney, *Curing the Mischiefs of Faction* (Berkeley: University of California Press, 1975).

17 Gary Orren, "The Nomination Process: Vicissitudes of Candidate Selection," in *The Elections of 1984,* ed. Michael Nelson (Washington, D.C.: CQ Press, 1985), 27–82.

18 Daniel Wirls, "Reinterpreting the Gender Gap," *Public Opinion Quarterly* 50 (1986): 316–30.

19 Adolph Reed, *The Jesse Jackson Phenomenon* (New Haven: Yale University Press, 1987).

20 Richard Scammon and Ben Wattenberg, *The Real Majority* (New York: Coward-McCann, 1970).

21 John Palmer and Isabel Sawhill, ed. *The Reagan Experiment* (Washington, D.C.: Urban Institute, 1982).

22 *New York Times,* 8 Nov. 1984, sec. A, p. 19.

23 *New York Times,* 10 Nov. 1988, sec. B, p. 6.

24 On the role of teachers' organizations in state Democratic campaigns, see Cornelius Cotter, James Gibson, John Bibby, and Robert Huckshorn, *Party Organizations in American Politics* (New York: Praeger, 1984), table 7.5.

25 Gary Jacobson, "Meager Patrimony: The Reagan Era and Republican Representation in Congress," in *Looking Back on the Reagan Presidency,* ed. Larry Berman (Baltimore: Johns Hopkins University Press, 1990).

26 Benjamin Ginsberg, "The New Political Economy of American Elections," in *The Political Economy,* ed. Thomas Ferguson and Joel Rogers (Armonk, N.Y.: M.E. Sharpe Publications, 1984); Gary Jacobson and Samuel Kernell, *Strategy and Choice in Congressional Elections,* 2nd ed. (New Haven: Yale University Press, 1983).

27 Brooks Jackson, *Honest Graft: Big Money and the American Political Process* (New York: Knopf, 1988).

CHAPTER 3

1 On the role of nonprofit organizations in the delivery of public services, see Lester M. Salamon, "Rethinking Public Management: Third Party Government and the Changing

Forms of Government Action," *Public Policy* 29 (Summer 1981): 255–75.

2   Joel Aberbach and Bert Rockman, "Clashing Beliefs Within the Executive Branch," *American Political Science Review* 70 (June 1976): 456–68.

3   Calculated from data on the votes of individuals in identifiably public sector occupations in the 1984 National Election Survey of the University of Michigan Center for Political Studies.

4   Theodore J. Lowi, *The End of Liberalism* (New York: W.W. Norton, 1979).

5   *New York Times*/CBS News 1988 presidential election exit poll, *New York Times,* 10 Nov. 1988, sec. B, p. 6.

6   Richard Polenberg, *Reorganizing Roosevelt's Government* (Cambridge, Mass.: Harvard University Press, 1966), 167; see also Peri Arnold, *Making the Managerial Presidency* (Princeton: Princeton University Press, 1986).

7   Civil Service Assembly, *Civil Service Agencies in the United States, A 1940 Census* (Washington, D.C.: U.S. Government Printing Office, 1940), pamphlet no. 16.

8   See Sidney Milkis, "The New Deal, Administrative Reform, and the Transcendence of Partisan Politics," *Administration and Society* 18 (January 1987): 433–72.

9   Elizabeth Sanders, "Business, Bureaucracy, and the Bourgeoisie: The New Deal Legacy," in *The Political Economy of Public Policy,* ed. Alan Stone and Edward Harpham (New York: Russell Sage Foundation, 1982), 115–42.

10 James Sundquist, *Dynamics of the Party System* (Washington, D.C.: Brookings Institution, 1983), chap. 11.

11 Stephen Erie, *Rainbow's End* (Berkeley and Los Angeles: University of California Press, 1988), chap. 4.

12 Martin Shefter, "Political Incorporation and the Extrusion of the Left: Party Politics and Social Forces in New York

City," *Studies in American Political Development* 1 (1986): 50–90.

13   John Fenton, *Midwest Politics* (New York: Holt, Rinehart and Winston, 1966), chaps. 2–3; see also Richard Valelly, *Radicalism in the States* (Chicago: University of Chicago Press, 1989).

14   David Mayhew, *Placing Parties in American Politics* (Princeton: Princeton University Press, 1986), chap. 2.

15   David Greenstone, *Labor in American Politics* (New York: Knopf, 1969). On the power of organized labor during the postwar period, see Karen Orren, "Union Politics and Postwar Liberalism in the United States, 1946–1979," *Studies in American Political Development* 1 (1986): 215–54.

16   Peter Marris and Martin Rein, *Dilemmas of Social Reform* (Chicago: Aldine, 1973); Frances Fox Piven and Richard A. Cloward, *Regulating the Poor* (New York: Pantheon, 1971), chap. 9.

17   Daniel Patrick Moynihan, *Maximum Feasible Misunderstanding* (New York: The Free Press, 1969), chap. 2; Samuel Beer, "The Modernization of American Federalism," *Publius* 3 (Fall 1973): 75.

18   Robert Salisbury, "Urban Politics: The New Convergence of Power," *Journal of Politics* 26 (November 1964): 775–97.

19   On the political mobilization of blacks through federal urban programs see Peter Eisinger, *The Politics of Displacement* (New York: Academic Press, 1980); Rufus Browning, Dale Rogers Marshall, and David Tabb, *Protest Is Not Enough* (Berkeley and Los Angeles: University of California Press, 1984).

20   Lewis Anthony Dexter, "Congressmen and the Making of Military Policy," in *New Perspectives on the House of Representatives,* ed. Robert Peabody and Nelson Polsby (Chicago: Rand McNally, 1963), 305–24.

21 David Vogel, *Fluctuating Fortunes* (New York: Basic Books, 1989), chaps. 3–5; James Q. Wilson, "The Politics of Regulation," in *The Politics of Regulation,* ed. James Q. Wilson (New York: Basic Books, 1980), 357–94.

22 See Charles O. Jones, *Clean Air* (Pittsburgh: University of Pittsburgh Press, 1975); Charles Noble, *Liberalism at Work* (Philadelphia: Temple University Press, 1986); Graham Wilson, *The Politics of Safety and Health* (Oxford: Clarendon Press, 1985).

23 Byron Shafer, *The Quiet Revolution* (New York: Russell Sage Foundation, 1985).

24 Nelson Polsby, *Consequences of Party Reform* (New York: Oxford University Press, 1983), chap. 2.

25 Jeremy Rabkin, *Judicial Compulsions* (New York: Basic Books, 1989).

26 Lawrence Dodd and Bruce Oppenheimer, "Consolidating Power in the House: The Rise of a New Oligarchy," in *Congress Reconsidered,* 4th ed., ed. Lawrence Dodd and Bruce Oppenheimer (Washington, D.C.: Congressional Quarterly Press, 1989), 39–64.

CHAPTER 4

1 William Schneider, "The Political Legacy of the Reagan Years," in *The Reagan Legacy,* ed. Sidney Blumenthal and Thomas Byrne Edsall (New York: Pantheon, 1988), 51–98.

2 Aaron Wildavsky, *The Politics of the Budgetary Process* (Boston: Little, Brown, 1964).

3 John Ferejohn, "Congress and Redistribution," in *Making Economic Policy in Congress,* ed. Allen Schick (Washington, D.C.: American Enterprise Institute, 1983).

4   Martha Derthick and Paul Quirk, *The Politics of Deregulation* (Washington, D.C.: The Brookings Institution, 1985).

5   Peter Gourevitch, *Politics in Hard Times* (Ithaca: Cornell University Press, 1986), chap. 4.

6   Thomas Byrne Edsall, *The New Politics of Inequality* (New York: W.W. Norton, 1985), chap. 3; see also Thomas Ferguson and Joel Rogers, *Right Turn* (New York: Hill and Wang, 1986).

7   For an account of this conflict by a committed supply-sider, see Paul Craig Roberts, *The Supply-Side Revolution* (Cambridge, Mass.: Harvard University Press, 1984), chaps. 6–7.

8   Theodore J. Lowi, *The End of Liberalism* (New York: W.W. Norton, 1979).

9   Mike Davis, *Prisoners of the American Dream* (London: Verso, 1986), chaps. 4–5.

10 William Greider, *Secrets of the Temple* (New York: Simon and Schuster, 1987).

11 1984 election data in this chapter are from the National Election Survey of the University of Michigan's Center for Political Studies. 1988 data are from the *New York Times/ CBS News* exit poll, *New York Times,* 10 Nov. 1988, sec. B, p. 6.

12 Steven Brint, "New Class and Cumulative Trend Explanations of the Liberal Political Attitudes of Professionals," *American Journal of Sociology* 90 (July 1984): 30–71.

13 Ira Katznelson, *City Trenches* (Chicago: University of Chicago Press, 1982); John Mollenkopf, *The Contested City* (Princeton: Princeton University Press, 1983), chap. 3.

14 Michael Goldfield, *The Decline of Organized Labor in the United States* (Chicago: University of Chicago Press, 1987).

15 Arthur Maass, "U.S. Prosecution of State and Local Officials," *Publius* 17 (Summer 1987); 195–230.

16 Connie Paige, *The Right to Lifers* (New York: Summit, 1983).

17   V. O. Key, Jr., *Southern Politics* (New York: Random House, 1949); see also J. Morgan Kousser, *The Shaping of Southern Politics* (New Haven: Yale University Press, 1974).

18   *New York Times,* 10 Nov. 1988, sec. B, p. 6. On the role of evangelicalism in the Republican coalition, see Gillian Peele, *Revival and Reaction* (New York: Oxford University Press, 1985).

19   Benjamin Ginsberg, *The Captive Public* (New York: Basic Books, 1986), chap. 4.

20   See Mike Mills, "Base Closings: The Political Pain Is Limited," *Congressional Quarterly Weekly Report* 26, no. 53 (31 Dec. 1988): 3625–29.

21   Robert Reich, "High Tech, a Subsidiary of Pentagon Inc.," *New York Times,* 28 May 1985, sec. A, p. 23.

22   Cf. Paul Peterson, "The New Politics of Deficits," in *The New Direction in American Politics,* ed. John Chubb and Paul Peterson (Washington, D.C.: The Brookings Institution, 1985), chap. 13. On the electoral uses of macroeconomic policy see Edward Tufte, *Political Control of the Economy* (Princeton: Princeton University Press, 1978); Douglas Hibbs, *The American Political Economy* (Cambridge, Mass.: Harvard University Press, 1987), chaps. 7–9.

23   Robert Gilpin, *The Political Economy of International Relations* (Princeton: Princeton University Press, 1987), chap. 8.

CHAPTER 5

1   Paul E. Peterson and Mark Rom, "Macroeconomic Policy-making: Who Is in Control?" in *Can the Government Govern?* (Washington, D.C.: The Brookings Institution, 1989), 139–84.

2   I. M. Destler, *American Trade Politics: System Under Stress* (Washington, D.C.: The Twentieth Century Fund, 1986).

3   Robert Gilpin, *The Political Economy of International Relations* (Princeton: Princeton University Press, 1987), 156–70.

4   I. M. Destler and C. Randall Henning, *Dollar Politics* (Washington, D.C.: Institute for International Economics, 1989), chap. 4.

5   Walter LaFeber, *The American Age: United States Foreign Policy at Home and Abroad Since 1750* (New York: W.W. Norton, 1989).

6   Benjamin Ginsberg, *The Captive Public* (New York: Basic Books, 1986), chap. 4.

7   Daniel Wirls, "Defense as Domestic Politics: National Security Policy and Domestic Alignments in the 1980s," (Ph.D. diss., Cornell University, 1988).

8   Pat Towell, "Scandal Highlights Dilemma of Defense Purchasing Process," *Congressional Quarterly Weekly Report* 46, no. 25 (25 June 1988): 1723–25.

9   For a discussion of the genesis of this condition, see William Saletan and Nancy Waltzman, "Marcus Welby, J.D.," *The New Republic,* 17 April 1988, 19–24.

10 L. Gordon Crovitz and Jeremy Rabkin, eds., *The Fettered Presidency* (Washington, D.C.: American Enterprise Institute, 1989) 15–116.

11 U.S. Congress, *Report of the Congressional Committees Investigating the Iran-Contra Affair* (New York: Random House, 1988), 37–329.

12 See, e.g., "Europe vs. Arms Control," *The Wall Street Journal,* 24 Oct. 1986, p. 28.

13 Steven Pressman, "Public Sympathy Proves Effective Shield for North Against Committee," *Congressional Quarterly Weekly Report* 45, no. 29 (18 July 1987): 1564–65.

14 This would appear to be consistent with one of Theodore J. Lowi's major points. See Theodore J. Lowi, *The Personal Presidency* (Ithaca: Cornell University Press, 1985).

15   Martin Shapiro, "The Supreme Court: From Warren to Burger," in *The New American Political System,* ed. Anthony King (Washington, D.C.: American Enterprise Institute, 1978), 179–212; see also Martin Shapiro, "Fathers and Sons: The Court, the Commentators and the Search for Values," in *The Burger Court: The Counter-Revolution That Wasn't,* ed. Vincent Blasi (New Haven: Yale University Press, 1983), 218–38.

16   Jeremy Rabkin, *Judicial Compulsions* (New York: Basic Books, 1989).

17   Mark Silverstein and Benjamin Ginsberg, "The Supreme Court and the New Politics of Judicial Power," *Political Science Quarterly* 102 (Fall 1987): 371–88.

18   The abortion decision is *Webster* v. *Reproductive Health Services* 109 S. Ct. 3040 (1989). Among the most important civil rights decisions are *Croson* v. *City of Richmond* 108 S. Ct. 1010 (1989); *Wards Cove Packing* v. *Atonio* 109 S. Ct. 2115 (1989); *Martin* v. *Wilks* 109 S. Ct. 2180 (1989); and *Patterson* v. *McLean Credit Union* 109 S. Ct. 2363 (1989).

19   See *INS* v. *Chadha,* 462 U.S. 919 (1983) and *Bowsher* v. *Synar,* 478 U.S. 714 (1986).

20   Jeremy Rabkin, "The Reagan Revolution Meets the Regulatory Labyrinth," in *Do Elections Matter?* ed. Benjamin Ginsberg and Alan Stone (Armonk, N.Y.: M.E. Sharpe, 1986), 221–39.

21   See Terry M. Moe, "The Politics of Bureaucratic Structure," in *Can the Government Govern?* ed. John Chubb and Paul Peterson (Washington, D.C.: Brookings Institution, 1989), 267–331.

22   Michael B. Wallace, "Out of Control: Congress and the Legal Services Corporation," in *The Fettered Presidency,* ed. L. Gordon Crovitz and Jeremy Rabkin (Washington, D.C.: American Enterprise Institute, 1989), 169–84.

23 Reed Irvine, Letter to the Editor, *New York Times,* 30 Dec. 1984, sec. D, p. 12.

24 Anthony Lewis, "The Lure of Power," *New York Times,* 22 June 1989, sec. A, p. 23.

CHAPTER 6

1 Cf. John Chubb and Paul Peterson, "American Political Institutions and the Problems of Governance," in *Can the Government Govern?* ed. John Chubb and Paul Peterson (Washington, D.C.: Brookings Institution, 1989), 1–43.

2 The enactment of a self-financing system of catastrophic health insurance for the elderly and of welfare reform legislation are also commonly regarded as major accomplishments of the second Reagan administration and the 100th Congress. However, the payroll tax on middle- and upper-income Medicare recipients that financed catastrophic coverage came under attack in Congress immediately after going into effect. And to secure the enactment of welfare reform, its sponsors had to greatly limit the work requirements for recipients of public assistance and to dramatically reduce expenditures for job training and childcare—to the point that the statute is unlikely to achieve its objectives. See Martin Tolchin, "Care of Elderly: Benefits That Backfired," *New York Times,* 21 July 1989, sec. A, p. 7; Mickey Kaus, "Revenge of the Softheads," *The New Republic,* 19 June 1989, 24–27.

3 "With 115 Nominations Awaiting Votes, Fingers Point Fast and Furious," *New York Times,* 28 Aug. 1989, sec. B, p. 6.

4 Margaret Levi, *Of Rule and Revenue* (Berkeley and Los Angeles: University of California Press, 1988), chap. 5.

5   Robert Gilpin, *The Political Economy of International Relations* (Princeton: Princeton University Press, 1987), 328–36.

6   William McNeill, *The Pursuit of Power* (Chicago: University of Chicago Press, 1982), chap. 3.

7   Barry Boyer and Errol Meidinger, "Privatizing Regulatory Enforcement," *Buffalo Law Review* 34 (1985): 833–956.

8   John Brewer, *The Sinews of Power: War, Money, and the English State, 1688–1783* (New York: Knopf, 1989), 93.

9   On the 1986 tax reform bill see Jeffrey Birnbaum and Alan Murray, *Showdown at Gucci Gulch* (New York: Random House, 1987).

10 David Stockman, *The Triumph of Politics* (New York: Harper & Row, 1986), 290.

11 Lloyd Cutler, "Now Is the Time for All Good Men . . . ," *William and Mary Law Review* 30 (Winter 1989): 387–402.

12 On the Social Security Commission see R. Kent Weaver, *Automatic Government* (Washington, D.C.: Brookings Institution, 1988), chap. 2; Paul Light, *Artful Work: The Politics of Social Security Reform* (New York: Random House, 1985).

13 See, for example, Bruce Ackerman and William Hassler, *Clean Coal/Dirty Air* (New Haven: Yale University Press, 1981); R. Shep Melnick, "Pollution Deadlines and the Coalition for Failure," *The Public Interest,* 75 (Spring 1984): 123–34.

14 See, for example, John Ferejohn and Charles Shipan, "Congressional Influence on Administrative Agencies: A Case Study of Telecommunications Policy," in *Congress Reconsidered,* 4th ed. (Washington, D.C.: Congressional Quarterly Press, 1989), 393–410; Barry Weingast and Mark Moran, "Bureaucratic Discretion or Congressional Control? Regulatory Policy-making by the Federal Trade Commission," *Journal of Political Economy* 91 (1983): 765–800.

15 Michael Wallace, "Out of Control: Congress and the Legal Services Corporation," in *The Fettered Presidency,* ed. L. Gordon Crovitz and Jeremy Rabkin (Washington, D.C.: American Enterprise Institute, 1989), 169–84.

16 Terry Moe, "The Politics of Bureaucratic Structure," in *Can the Government Govern?* ed. John Chubb and Paul Peterson (Washington, D.C.: Brookings Institution, 1989), 289–97.

17 Gary Bryner, *Bureaucratic Discretion* (New York: Pergamon Press, 1987).

18 Louis Fisher, "Micromanagement by Congress: Reality and Mythology," in *The Fettered Presidency,* ed. L. Gordon Crovitz and Jeremy Rabkin (Washington, D.C.: American Enterprise Institute, 1989), 151.

19 Benjamin Friedman, *Day of Reckoning* (New York: Random House, 1988); cf. Robert Eisner, *How Real Is the Federal Deficit?* (New York: The Free Press, 1986).

20 Henry Aaron et al., *Economic Choices 1987* (Washington, D.C.: Brookings Institution, 1986), 22.

21 John E. Chubb, "U.S. Energy Policy: A Problem of Delegation," in *Can the Government Govern?* ed. John Chubb and Paul Peterson (Washington, D.C.: Brookings Institution, 1989), 80–86.

22 Stephen Skowronek, *Building a New American State* (New York: Cambridge University Press, 1982), chaps. 6–8.

23 Richard L. McCormick, "The Discovery That Business Corrupts Politics: A Reappraisal of the Origins of Progressivism," *American Historical Review* 86 (April 1981): 247–74.

24 Frances Fox Piven and Richard A. Cloward, *Why Americans Don't Vote* (New York: Pantheon, 1988), chap 3; cf. Philip Converse, "Change in the American Electorate," in *The Human Meaning of Social Change,* ed. Angus Campbell and Philip Converse (New York: Russell Sage Foundation, 1972), 263–301.

25   Walter Dean Burnham, *The Current Crisis in American Politics* (New York: Oxford University Press, 1982), chaps. 1–2, 4; Paul R. Abramson and John H. Aldrich, "The Decline of Electoral Participation in America," *American Political Science Review* 76 (September 1982): 502–21; Raymond Wolfinger and Steven Rosenstone, *Who Votes?* (New Haven: Yale University Press, 1980).

26   Eric McKitrick, "Party Politics and the Union and Confederate War Efforts," in *The American Party Systems,* ed. William Nisbet Chambers and Walter Dean Burnham (New York: Oxford University Press, 1967), 117–51.

27   See the essays in Margaret Weir, Ann Orloff, and Theda Skocpol, eds., *The Politics of Social Policy in the United States* (Princeton: Princeton University Press, 1988).

28   Kristi Anderson, *The Creation of a Democratic Majority, 1928–1936* (Chicago: University of Chicago Press, 1979).

29   David Plotke, "The Wagner Act, Again: Politics and Labor, 1935–37," *Studies in American Political Development* 3 (1988): 105–56.

30   See, for example, Joseph Califano, Jr., "Tough Talk for Democrats," *The New York Times Magazine,* 8 Jan. 1989, 28–43. See also Dan Balz, "Democrats Urged to End 'Evasion,'" *Washington Post,* 8 Sept. 1989, sec. A, p. 8.

31   Max Farrand, ed., *The Records of the Federal Convention of 1787,* vol. 1 (New Haven: Yale University Press, 1966), 49.

32   James DeNardo, "Turnout and the Vote: The Joke's on the Democrats," *American Political Science Review* 70 (June 1980): 406–20.

33   John P. Diggins, *The Proud Decades: America in War and Peace, 1941–1960* (New York: W.W. Norton, 1988), 21.

Index

Natural Resources Defense Council, 93

New Deal, 19, 22, 58, 60, 79, 80–83; coalition, 37, 38, 41, 95, 115; and the middle class, 95; regulatory programs, 93, 106; system, challenges to, 44–47, 63

New Frontier, 41–42, 86, 87

News media, 23–26, 30–31, 52, 61, 68, 159; and institutional combat, 156, 159–60; "investigative reporting," 24, 96; and Iran-contra, 144–45, 146; leaks to, 23, 27, 34, 80; and Quayle's nomination, 69; and RIP attacks, 35; and Watergate, 27–28. *See also* Newspapers; Television

Newspapers, 9, 22, 23, 25–26. *See also* specific newspapers

Newsweek, 27

New York Times, 160; CBS News exit polls, 68, 201n5, 204n11; and the Pentagon Papers, 27; and the Vietnam War, 23; and Watergate, 27; and the Wright affair, 31

Nicaragua, 33, 139, 143, 167. *See also* Iran-contra scandal

Nie, Norman, 199n14

Nixon, Richard, 16, 54, 63–64, 65, 96, 97; and Watergate, 27–28, 146, 147–48. *See also* Nixon administration

Nixon administration, 42, 179;

and the federal judiciary, 27, 146, 148, 152, 153–54; and the media, 24, 27–28; and RIP weaponry, 26–28

Noble, Charles, 203n22

Nofziger, Lyn, 4–5, 160

Noonan, John, 154

Noriega, Manuel, 35

North, Oliver, 5, 143, 145, 147

Nuclear freeze, 107, 141

Nuclear power industry, 45, 183

O'Connor, Sandra Day, 154

Office of Management and Budget (OMB), 17, 156, 165

OPEC (Organization of Petroleum Exporting Countries), 43

Oppenheimer, Bruce, 203n26

Orloff, Ann, 211n27

Ornstein, Norman, 166

Orren, Gary, 199n17

Orren, Karen, 202n15

Page, Benjamin, 198n3

Paige, Connie, 204n16

Palmer, John, 200n21

Peele, Gillian, 205n18

Pentagon Papers, 24, 27, 152

Persian Gulf, 43, 139, 143

Peterson, Paul E., 205n1, 205n22, 208n1